THE PARTY
of YOUR LIFE

Get the Funeral You Want by Planning It Yourself

Erika Dillman

Published by: Santa Monica Press LLC
P.O. Box 850
Solana Beach, CA 92075
1-800-784-9553
www.santamonicapress.com
books@santamonicapress.com

Printed in the United States

Santa Monica Press books are available at special quantity discounts
when purchased in bulk by corporations, organizations, or groups.
Please call our Special Sales department at 1-800-784-9553.

ISBN-13 978-1-59580-062-6

Library of Congress Cataloging-in-Publication Data

Dillman, Erika.
 The party of your life : get the funeral you want by planning it yourself /
by Erika Dillman.
    p. cm.
 ISBN 978-1-59580-062-6
 1. Funeral rites and ceremonies—United States. I. Title.
 GT3203.D55 2011
 393'.9–dc22

                            2008004279

Cover and interior design and production by Future Studio

"I have found that, as in all grave situations of life, two things are most useful: a common-sense approach and a sense of humor."

—SOGYAL RINPOCHE (1947–), Buddhist teacher, from *The Tibetan Book of Living and Dying*

CONTENTS

Death Becomes Me

Why I Started Planning My Funeral at 40

*Y*ou might say that death becomes me. Or that I'm completely self-obsessed. From a very young age I've been acutely aware of possessing the genes to outlast my peers, while at the same time feeling a need to prepare for the worst.

I come from a long line of hearty Swedish farmwomen, pioneers who came to America in the early 1900s. They worked hard, drank a lot of gin, and, for the most part, lived long, productive lives. My grandmother, who outlived all of her nine siblings as well as her husband's entire family, lived to 99. Her older sister, my great Aunt Eva, lived to 102. (Another sister, my great aunt Signe, only lived to 82 . . . but she never took care of herself.)

My father's people weren't necessarily blessed with longevity genes—although his mother lived to a respectable 92—but they knew everything about death. His grandparents owned a funeral home, which they operated in the basement of a furniture store, and his father sold funeral supplies (a business my grandmother carried on long after he died and well into her eighties.)

My paternal grandparents talked about death all the time. It was a preoccupation for them, a business, and simply one of those life responsibilities you had to take care of, like having car insurance. From as early as I can remember, I knew that funerals were important matters requiring thoughtful planning. I also knew exactly what would happen to my body when I died. These are things you learn when your grandparents peddle embalming fluid.

When I was eight years old, my grandparents took me to a funeral convention, where I picked out my own casket: a baby blue model with silver handles. I thought it was the fanciest box in the room, much nicer than the staid mahogany casket my grandmother picked for herself. There were so many options—all so shiny and regal. Death seemed so dignified. I knew then that I was going to have a great funeral.

As I got older, I spent less time with my death-obsessed grandparents and discovered a taste for gin. So, I didn't think much about death again until I was in my thirties. When I was bored, or alone, or on long walks in the park, I often found myself eulogizing my close friends in my head, mentally composing their obituaries as a way to recall all the good times we had shared.

I also enjoyed wondering how I might be eulogized. What would my friends say about me? What would they wear? What kind of music would they play? Who would be the saddest? Would it be fair to my guests to stick to my vegan principles at my funeral fête since I wouldn't be there to eat any of the food anyway?

With time I realized I couldn't be happy leaving my end-of-life celebration(s) up in the air. What if I died young? My mother wouldn't know whom to invite. I had to start planning now; I was almost 40. At this point, I was so over the blue casket, preferring cremation and a fancy bejeweled urn instead, but I did want to have a funeral that people would be dying to attend.

Once I'd recovered from all the hoopla surrounding my 40th birthday (a season of celebrations lasting three months and taking place in two states), I took advantage of the lingering buzz from my parties to recruit my funeral team (you can't pull off a truly fantastic funeral without a lot of help from loyal friends). Of course, it wasn't long before my mother, who has nothing to do with the funeral business, heard about my plans and asked me for help planning her own end-of-life celebration. So I started writing this book.

The Parties of Their Lives

Throughout the course of this project, I've been encouraged by feedback from friends, family members, acquaintances, neighbors, the young man at the tea shop, strangers who were unlucky enough to be seated next to me on airplanes, every stylist who's cut my hair in the past six years, the seamstress who hemmed my favorite black pants, and even my pharmacist.

Every time I mentioned the topic of my book, each one of them launched into a funeral story, usually about a relative's funeral that had left them unsatisfied or upset or that they felt had been mishandled. Their comments were always followed by a list of what they wanted for their own exits: more control, more merriment, and a more celebration-oriented attitude. Some of these folks were nice enough to share their fantastic funeral plans with me, so I've included them here. (In some cases I've changed names, dates, or locations to protect privacy.) I've enjoyed hearing about all of these funeral party plans; I've also been inspired by the changes that are happening in the funeral business.

As you'll read later in the book, we all have many more choices now thanks to a growing group of individuals and organizations dedicated to demystifying the funeral process and educating people about more natural death care services, lower-cost disposal options, and family-directed funerals. Now funeral consumers can learn how to shop for the best deals—and how to select only the end-of-life services and products they need—so they can plan affordable, personalized exits.

I hope this book helps you get the funeral you want and deserve!

ERIKA DILLMAN

INTRODUCTION

Your Day, Your Way

The Party of Your Life

*H*ave you ever wondered what kind of funeral you'd get if you died tomorrow? I have. I've thought about it a lot, and I've decided not to leave the details of my last big bash up to chance. My survivors need my input now, before it's too late.

Let me be clear—I plan on living to 100, but accidents do happen. I could be crushed by falling debris or hit by a bus tomorrow, and who would know that I want Nina Simone played at my wake or black cod with edamame pesto served at my funeral banquet?

Faced with the possibility of such an untimely death (not to mention the unacceptable notion of a slapdash funeral arranged in the chaotic hours following my demise), I have created a comprehensive end-of-life plan and appointed a team of trusted friends to make sure I get the funeral I want and deserve.

I'm a firm believer in the saying "If you want something done right, do it yourself." I'm also pragmatic. Death is a bummer, but it's the one sure thing in life. The way I see it, you're better off accepting it and going out in style with an event designed to celebrate *you, you, you*, as well as entertain your loved ones. And who better to plan a party all about you than you?

You Can Go Your Own Way

Frankly, there's never been a better time to die. Thanks to baby boomers, who have applied their "me, me, me" approach to every aspect of life and, now, to death, the funeral industry is adapting to meet their (your) unique memorial needs. Gloomy funerals are out; personalized life celebrations rule the day. In fact, many people are skipping funerals in favor of memorial parties.

Your funeral can be a colorful, festive occasion, or a simple, family-directed farewell in the comfort of your own home. If you're like me, you might feel that your life is just too big for a single funeral function. You (and your guests) may need several days, a week, or even a month of remembrance events. Get started now by starring in your own memory video, which your survivors can later distribute to your guests or upload to your funeral website, and by compiling your funeral soundtrack on iTunes. Funeral directors, clergy, death midwives, home funeral guides, celebrants, and a variety of "end-trepreneurs" are standing by to help you and your survivors realize your funeral vision.

Goodbye to You

By planning ahead, you get to relive a lot of wonderful memories, spend time focusing on yourself, and reduce the drama and strain on your family and friends during the most painful time of their lives. Most important, you'll be able to rest in peace knowing that your survivors understand your last wishes. (And you can bank on the fact that they'll feel duty-bound to carry out even your most whimsical celebratory schemes.)

Wouldn't you like to have a magnificent exit that reflects

your interests, achievements, and good taste?

The Party of Your Life will help you explore the full range of creative, culinary, musical, and theatrical possibilities of a well-planned (i.e. self-planned) life celebration. This book is for anyone who wants to say goodbye in his or her own special way. It's also for control freaks like me, who don't trust their survivors to throw them the funeral to end all funerals.

INSTRUCTIONS

Getting the Funeral You Want and Deserve

How to Use This Book

The key to planning a successful life celebration is accepting that your funeral should be all about you. This doesn't make you selfish; it just means that you have standards, as well as the good manners to show your survivors a really good time on what will be a very difficult day for them. You shouldn't need to be reminded that you are special and so worth a unique send-off.

It's also critical to share your plans with your friends and family. Discuss your last wishes often, and in detail, so that everyone knows what you want (and especially what you don't want) when the time comes.

Read All About It

If you haven't already, scan the table of contents and skim through the chapters to get an idea of the big picture and the various tasks ahead. This book is packed with real-life examples and anecdotes to inspire you to exit with style—your style. At the end of each chapter you'll find a short checklist of steps to guide you in your preparations.

There's also a detailed outline summarizing essential pre-planning tasks, called "Do Before I Die: *Your Quickie Party Checklist*" in the appendix, page 249. Photocopy the list and tape it to your refrigerator to help you stay on task!

If you're young, healthy, and safety-conscious, you probably have a great chance of finishing this book and completing your funeral planning long before your time is up, so read the chapters in order to avoid missing any important information.

However, if the clock is ticking, or if you're dying to dive into dinner menus and decoration ideas, you might want to skip ahead to the sections that are most important to you.

Write All About It

Because you won't be around to host the party of your life, you need to leave behind clear instructions for your survivors.

Keep a pen and paper handy while reading, so you can jot down ideas, demands, requests, and preferences. It's always a good idea to have a few small, manageable action steps in place so you're covered if you fall off of a cliff while hiking next weekend.

You can use my free funeral-planning worksheets, available for download at www.thepartyofyourlife.com, to help you organize vital information about yourself, highlight specific party details, and record end-of-life decisions.

Your Funeral Box

Keep all of your planning materials in a safe but findable place, and don't forget to tell a few people where they are. If you're organized, you can use a filing cabinet, although you might want to designate a drawer or a small box for storing bulky items.

Your funeral box doesn't need to be elaborate (I use an old

hiking boot box), but it should have enough room to hold your planning worksheets, architectural drawings of potential party venues, sample funeral T-shirt designs, your remembrance DVD, and any other items your survivors may need to produce the party of your life.

If you'll be writing your plans on your computer, save all of your funeral files into a folder called, "My Funeral Party Plans," and leave a note in your box describing where your survivors can find the files on your hard drive. (Or, if you use an online funeral planning site, leave the account information in your box.) Better still, print hard copies for your box whenever you update your plans, and back up your files on a media storage device (along with your funeral photos and music), which you can also store in your box. Your will is NOT the place to describe your funeral wishes or end-of-life decisions; you'll be long gone before anyone reads it.

When I die, my survivors will have no trouble locating my funeral box because I have already attached a short note describing its location to my refrigerator with an "In Case I Die" magnet. Post-me, my loved ones can decorate my funeral box and convert it into a memorial container for storing locks of my hair, photos of me, and other talismans and mementos. If you're close to perishing, you might want to leave copies of your plans with at least two trustworthy friends or relatives.

Share the Fun

The Party of Your Life will provide you with many enjoyable hours of self-focus, as well as the satisfaction of leaving your affairs in order before you're too ill, feeble, or dead to make your own decisions about how you should be celebrated. While you're at it, invite your spouse or partner, and even your children, to form a funeral prep workshop. Imagine the fun you can have spending an afternoon or weekend together, brainstorming party ideas and developing event concepts for your one-of-a-kind memorial.

If you need more time, form a *Party of Your Life* book club and meet weekly with a small group of trusted friends to work through a chapter or two at a time. In this case, take care selecting each group member, and you might want to keep your best ideas to yourself so nobody is tempted to copy them. A lot of your valuable time could go to waste if a friend steals your concepts and dies first.

What's in a Name?

Finally, whenever you see the word "funeral" in these pages, keep in mind that I use this term generically to describe whatever type of final event or events you choose to celebrate yourself. "Funeral" can mean a service, a memorial party, a graveside ceremony, an ash-scattering, a wake or visitation, a remembrance lineup that includes all of these events (or none of these events), or *your* adaptation of any or all of these occasions.

In case you have any lingering doubts or fears about getting the funeral you want and deserve—you can let go of any superstitious feelings you might have about pre-planning your funeral. Thinking about it and planning it will not signal to the universe that you're ready to go. You're not that powerful, and it just doesn't happen that way. Thousands of people plan funerals every day, and they're still walking around, living their lives. It's a party. It won't kill you.

"They say such nice things about people at their funerals that it makes me sad to realize I'm going to miss mine by just a few days."

—GARRISON KEILLOR (1942–),
author, radio storyteller, and host of *A Prairie Home Companion* and *The Writer's Almanac*

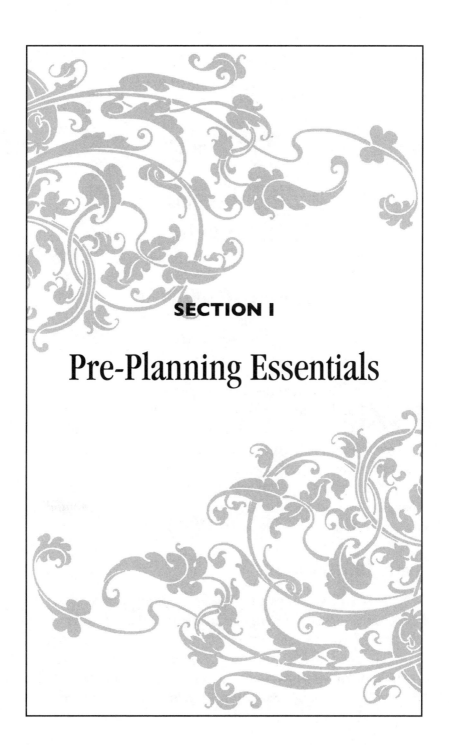

SECTION I

Pre-Planning Essentials

CHAPTER I

Putting the "F-U-N" Back in Funeral

The Benefits of Self-Planning

unerals are the new weddings. They're rich in festive and dramatic possibilities, and they bring together all of your loved ones. Best of all, your funeral is *your* day, and it's all about you. You get to select the menu, you get to invite whomever you want, you get to pick the music.

Your funeral is your last chance to express your best self, make a few demands, care for your loved ones, and say goodbye on your own terms.

Party Like It's 1999

So what makes a funeral fun? Pageantry, pomp, party favors, processions, parades, interactive rituals involving fire and water, contests of wit and strength, exotic food, rich cakes and custards, intrigue, good music, the drunken, sort-of-inappropriate-but-basically-harmless guest nobody seems to know but was clearly invited (or was he?), quality gin, dancing, and more food—the same things that make other parties and milestone events fun.

Having a spectacular send-off isn't a new concept; throughout history, cultures around the world have honored and celebrated the dead with a variety of engaging funeral rites. Ancient Aztec and Mayan Indians held graveside feasts and decorated cemeteries with colorful flowers. Wealthy Romans made sure their funeral festivities stayed festive by hiring professional dancers to regale attendees. Pagan Irish funerals were lively affairs, featuring choruses of singing mourners and funeral games involving athletic feats. In Korea, *Dasiraegi*, a traditional play featuring folk songs and dances, remains a revered tradition.

With so much history and so many new celebration possibilities, you should have no trouble designing a one-of-a-kind send-off. It's never too early to start planning. Researching and identifying your funeral goals now, while you're alive and healthy, can help you determine the most effective and captivating ways to highlight *you* and your fabulous life.

The Times They Are A-Changin'

For too long, funerals have gotten a bad rap. That's because the traditional American funeral service is inherently sad, depressing, and unoriginal.

Most often, it's held at a church or funeral home chapel, featuring the usual scripture readings, the same old tired hymns, and somber organ music (which, by the way, is the saddest sad death music ever and kind of manipulative when you think about it). Too quiet, too solemn, too stiff.

Afterward, a reception: polite chitchat and finger food made out of white bread and mayonnaise. How boring. What could an event like that possibility say to your loved ones about *you* and your life? Not much. Then there's the price tag. A bland little event such as this, the average funeral, costs between $6,000 and $8,000 (more like $10,000 if you add burial and cemetery costs, and other death merch). That doesn't even include memorial bookmarks, invitations, mourning outfits, and other "extras." No wonder people cry.

Let the Good Times Roll

There's nothing wrong with a little veneration, but what about celebration? How about some relief from all the grief?

Remember how you got goosebumps during the funeral scene in *The Big Chill*, when the septuagenarian organist laid down the first few chords of "You Can't Always Get What You Want"? If you want your guests to immediately connect with you and with each other, you have to set the tone from beat one.

Hymns are so ho-hum. Lively up yourself with "Rock the Casbah" and "Baba O'Riley," slip in some Billie Holliday for some atmosphere, then shimmy it out with "Queen Bitch." That'll get your guests rockin' and let them know that you're dead serious about having them celebrate your life.

Ditch the gloomy venue. Swap the lilies for a laser light show. Recruit an officiate with a fresh approach to sacred observances—whatever will breathe life (your life) into the festivities. Out with the old, in with the you.

It's your choice. Do you want a sedate, cookie-cutter funeral or a funtastic party of your life?

Well-Planned = Self-Planned

It's not enough to simply die anymore. You need a festive farewell that embodies your sunny spirit, showcases your unique character, and inspires your survivors.

Have a funeral, have a memorial party, have a small funeral followed a month later by a raucous remembrance roller derby. Have as many or as few events as you wish. Just be original. With personalized life celebrations becoming more popular, your guests will expect as much.

Too many people have missed out on having fantastic

funerals because they didn't plan ahead. Maybe they didn't know they could, or maybe they just didn't take responsibility for their post-life plans. Maybe they never considered the possibility that an untimely death could happen to them.

It's Up to You

If you do nothing about your funeral, your survivors will inevitably turn to the "professionals"—i.e., funeral directors and clergy—for guidance, when they should have your database of event planners, vegan caterers, glitter specialists, and dance coaches. Then you'll either end up with a beige little funeral, or worse, your memorial will be mishandled by meddling relatives. Do you really want your mother picking out your funeral outfit? Or your weird cousin Benny reading his cat poetry at your service?

I'm not saying that there aren't funeral directors and clergy members out there who couldn't step up and (help) throw a remarkable funeral, but they may not go there on their own. Without your vision spelled out to the letter, and an assertive celebration team managing your funeral plans, your relatives, as well-meaning as they might be, might very likely plan a memorial that says more about them than about you. Why? For the same reason your aunt always gives you acrylic reindeer sweaters every Christmas: people tend to give what they think you'd want, which is actually what they'd want.

There's nothing more depressing than a bad funeral, especially now, when there are so many exciting departure options. You can get more bang for your buck and show your guests the time of their lives (and your life) by pre-planning your last big bash.

You owe it to yourself and your guests, many of whom may have to fly across the country for your funeral, to make your last party your best party.

Benefits of the DIY Funeral

There are so many good reasons to plan your own funeral. Aside from the glaringly obvious creative issues, planning the party of your life gives you control and your survivors direction during a very traumatic time for all you.

In the painful hours and days following your demise, your loved ones will need all the help they can get. Your detailed party plan will give them something to do and help ease their pain. They'll be so busy trying to fulfill your last wishes that they won't have time to mope. Pre-planning gives you the chance to:

- Script and shape the event(s).
- Recruit a funeral team to carry out your wishes.
- Research the professionals who can bring your funeral dreams to life.
- Select an appropriate venue.
- Decide on a disposal method that meets your spiritual needs, environmental standards, and celebration timeline.

It also gives you time to destroy any embarrassing or incriminating photos, memos, emails, or other information that could surface after your death. You may be able to take some secrets with you to the grave, but others will inevitably be exposed (and cause your loved ones a lot of pain) if you don't tie up loose ends now. For example, if you have a secret family in another state, now might be a better time for all of your loved ones to meet than at your funeral (this actually happened to a friend of mine). It's your mess; clean it up before you go!

Cleaner, Leaner, Greener

Pre-planning your funeral can help you save money and the earth. Today, many people want a simpler, more affordable, and more meaningful exit. They also want more control over end-of-life events. Home-based, family-directed funerals and green burials are becoming popular choices as consumers seek out less invasive death care and eco-friendly exits.

By skipping some traditional and unnecessary funeral products, such as embalming and a casket, you can trim some fat off of that $10K funeral price tag. Keep it simple and depart in a shroud or a biodegradable cardboard burial vessel that your friends can decorate at your home death vigil.

I'm not suggesting you skimp on your funeral and related events, but rather, think about how you want to allocate your funds. Why pay for things you don't need when you can throw a funeral bash that will provide your loved ones with hours, if not days, of fun and remembrance? Your funeral isn't just about reliving old memories, but creating new memories, too, so that you will live on in your survivors' hearts and minds forever.

The thousands of dollars you can save by being a smart consumer or, better, by skipping some unnecessary death care services in favor of an eco farewell, could pay for the multi-media presentation in your Memory Room, a champagne brunch for your inner circle, or iPhones for your funeral team members. The karmic energy you'll create by returning to Mother Earth in a natural, non-polluting way—well, you can't put a price tag on that.

Express Yourself

Most important, self-planning your funeral allows you to celebrate yourself and let your loved ones know who you were and what was important to you.

Use the party of your life to celebrate a life-long hobby, profession, or obsession, as did the Pittsburgh Steelers fan who had his survivors stage his viewing at home so his friends could see him indulging in his favorite pastime: sitting in a reclining chair, Steelers blanket across his lap, "watching" a pre-recorded loop of his favorite team. Or, if you only have a few months to live, throw yourself a "going away" party like a woman in Washington did. Surrounded by 40 friends and harp music, she entertained her guests dressed in an angel costume, complete with gossamer wings and halo.

You can also use your last bash to reveal a side of yourself that didn't get much play in life . . . or simply arrange to go out with a bang. A Lutheran pastor from Minnesota, who my friend, a former member of his parish (and his nephew), affectionately refers to as "the blaster pastor," requested that his ashes be mixed into fireworks and exploded over the St. Croix River on the 4th of July. Journalist Hunter S. Thompson took a less sparkly and more direct approach when his ashes where shot out of a cannon in the mountains near his Colorado home.

Your end-of-life celebration(s) is also a chance to showcase

THE PARTY *of* JOANNE DILLMAN'S LIFE

JOANNE DILLMAN
1939–
Illinois, USA

PARTY:	I don't want a funeral, just a party. It will be open to all. I'd like it to be informal. If people would like to toast me or reminisce, say a few words, that would be nice.
SOUNDTRACK:	I'd like an evening of Swedish music—polkas and schottisches so people can dance. I'd like one of my friends, either Dalia or Zenia, to sing "Amazing Grace."
FOOD:	A traditional Swedish smorgasbord (pickled

hidden talents, reveal lifelong secrets, and even accomplish what you never did in life. Maybe you haven't thought of it before, but even in death, you still have the chance to help your survivors learn more about you, which can only further endear you to them. You can finally give out your secret chili recipe. In fact, have it printed on the back of the menu at your funeral barbecue.

Dig out your old 4-H ribbons from the state fair and your high school track trophies. Your friends will get a kick out of your old yearbooks, too, so don't forget those. Get creative with your mementos. What about a collage or photo mural of your hairdos throughout the years? Your past—even the bad hair days—is a rich source of entertainment for them, because it's their past, too.

	herring, salmon, pickled beets, pickled cucumbers, ham, potatoes, Swedish meatballs, etc.).
DRINKS:	Aquavit to start the program, gin and tonics for the rest of the evening.
DISPOSAL:	No viewing. No embalming. I'd like to be buried in a simple but well-made pine box to honor my father, who was a carpenter. I'd like to be buried in the same cemetery in Michigan where my parents and aunts and uncles are. If my husband should predecease me, I would like some of his ashes in my coffin. Should I depart first, I would like some of his ashes placed in a small container on my grave.
LEGAL:	I have a medical directive and medical power of attorney in place.

Let the Healing Begin

M aybe you're not so sure you can pull this off. Maybe a little voice in the back of your head is telling you that it's selfish to plan your own funeral. Well, it's not. And you're not alone. More people are self-planning because they want and deserve a more personal, more expressive final fête than the traditional American funeral (and because it's fun). Don't worry; just plan.

Your guests won't deny you your special day or judge the depth of your self-focus in orchestrating what will be an action-packed day (or days) of good memories, good times, and even better gin. They'll find your attention to detail and your unorthodox requests charming and refreshing. In fact, they'll feel comforted knowing that you got the funeral you wanted and justified in wanting their own spectacular send-offs.

You only die once, so why not make the best of it?

Start Planning Now

You sparkled in life—why settle for a humdrum funeral? Do yourself and your survivors a big favor and start planning the party of your life now. Start by telling your survivors more about yourself.

- Download your planning worksheets from www.the partyofyourlife.com.

- Describe your spirituals beliefs, likes and dislikes, significant relationships, and anything else that will help your survivors know more about you and how to fête you.

- Identify the traits and qualities for which you'd like to be remembered.

- Identify the bad habits, outstanding debts, and illegal activities you'd like your survivors to keep secret for as long as possible.

- Store information in your funeral box.

CHAPTER 2

It Takes a Village

Your Funeral Posse

*S*ince you won't be there to make sure you get the funeral you want and deserve, you need to recruit a team of trusted friends and end-of-life professionals—your funeral posse—to carry out your plans once you're gone.

Why a Team?

It might seem premature to assemble a team before you've finished, or even started, planning the party of your life, but it depends on how you leave and whom you leave behind. If you're struck by lightning tomorrow, would you rather have your first-choice celebration advocates arrange your funeral without your input or leave behind a fabulous plan that someone not of your choosing could ignore or fumble?

I named my team (and alternates) years ago because if the worst happens before I'm done planning, I know my people will be on the job. Your friends love you. Use that to your advantage, and recruit your team now (before they get recruited to someone else's team!).

A Little Help from Your Friends

Selecting the right team can mean the difference between a mediocre memorial that barely resembles your dream send-off, and a dream-come-true funeral that'll do you proud.

I recommend recruiting friends and professionals in the business (of death and of event planning) as your key players, rather than family members. Your friends won't be attached to who you were when you were 10 or have an image of you that's complete fantasy. They know the best and worst of you, will take your most embarrassing secrets with them to their graves, and will be dedicated to fulfilling your funeral wishes. Plus, unlike siblings, they're much less likely to have private agendas or squabble among themselves about how to proceed.

Another bonus of a friends-only team: in the unlikely occurrence that you die before your parents, it would be nice if, for once, they didn't have to clean up after you. With a solid team handling the arrangements, all your parents have to do is pick out their celebration outfits and get to the party on time.

I've selected a handful of my closest friends to serve on my team, and I have complete faith in them. They know me best, they're used to accommodating my quirky demands, and they've already been tested. They did a fabulous job following the plans I gave them for my bi-coastal 40th birthday parties. I know my team will bring my funeral plans to life, and I trust them to make adjustments where necessary.

Of course, if you have a spouse you love and trust, you may want her or him to lead, or at least serve on, your team. On the other hand, if you're stuck in a bad marriage, you might want to talk to a lawyer to see if you have the option of naming someone else to be your designated agent in case you die before resolving your marriage woes or getting divorced (laws vary from state to state). That way, if you die in relationship limbo your embittered/ estranged/deranged spouse can't ruin your final day or just blow it off without any fêting at all. Maybe you and your ex had an amicable parting, but never got divorced . . . and now you're two years into a new relationship. Take care of any pending legal issues now, or your new love could end up unable to make important end-of-life decisions for you and be excluded from your funeral.

Who's Your Buddy?

If you can't come up with a complete team, that's okay. Maybe you don't have that many friends, or your friends simply aren't trustworthy enough to produce your dream funeral. Maybe you'll outlive all of your potential team members. Maybe you're not as demanding as I am.

Don't worry about these details now. Just focus on putting the "F-U-N" back in your funeral. If assembling a team seems too overwhelming, then select a single celebration advocate—your Death Buddy—who will go to your home, find your funeral box, and stand by your side until you end up where you want to end up.

Remember, the purpose of this book is to help you clarify how you want to go. If you need to keep it simple because you don't know who will be around to carry out your plans, you can still have a super send-off.

Hired Help

Whether you designate a single celebration advocate or re- cruit a full-on funeral posse, your survivors will probably appreciate some professional guidance to produce the party of your life. That's what party planners, photographers, videogra- phers, choreographers, and DJs are for!

Your team members will probably be happy to have a pro- fessional take care of your more mundane planning tasks. They'd rather interview massage therapists for your Relaxation Room and pick out the Mardi Gras beads for your funeral parade than sit in the stuffy lobby at the county registrar's office, waiting to file your death certificate. Go ahead and dream big, but when it comes to your to-do list, be practical and delegate appropriately. (And remember—you don't have to spend a lot of money to have a festive farewell party. See Chapter 5 for a list of celebration ideas for all budgets.)

Remember the "end-trepreneurs" mentioned on page 12? Well, thanks to the new face of death, funeral directors and clergy aren't your only options anymore. There are many end-of-life providers who can help you (or your team) get the funeral party you want and deserve. Celebrants can plan and officiate memorial parties and ceremonial functions, including a service, if you choose to have one. Home funeral guides can help your survivors host a home visitation, as well as a home funeral. There are even funeral concierge services that will make all of your end-of-life arrangements for you. Plus, you can shop for funeral merch and services online; your eco-friendly coffin or ornamental urn are just a just a few clicks away. (See Chapters 15 and 21 for information on celebrants, home funeral guides, and death midwives.)

For now, concentrate on selecting a devoted posse who will throw you the funeral you're dying to have.

Recruiting Your Dream Team

As you assemble your team, be critical and keep your funeral goals in mind. You don't want "nice" people. You want professional, assertive, won't-take-no-for-an-answer types who can get things done on time, on budget, and with a minimum of fuss. You want people who will make sure that the sausage appetizers don't touch the vegan nut rolls because that's the way you'd want it.

Here are your key players:

The Celebration Master: Boss and Vision Keeper
You need a Celebration Master (basically, your acting funeral

director) who can quickly pick up the reins when you die and get the show on the road. Your CM will oversee every detail of your demise, from your last breath to your final resting place. Obviously, you want a smart, creative, and—most important—loyal friend for this job.

You can't entrust the party of your life to just anyone. It has to be someone who understands your funeral vision, is dedicated

---

THE PARTY *of* NANCY LEE'S LIFE

NANCY LEE
1965–
California, USA

EVENT: I'd like to have a traditional New Orleans-style jazz funeral. Slow, mournful brass and drums playing as the band and the people walk behind the casket. (Although, in a slight break with tradition, I'd prefer to be carried in an urn.) Then, suddenly, the band will jump into an upbeat, joyful number and the second line—the people walking behind the band—will jump, swing, and dance with joy and abandon. I want booties shaking to that irresistible second-line beat. I would like people to dance like this for their own joy, and to remember what brought me joy.

ENERGY: It's the beat of a Mardi Gras parade. A party. The funkiest funk. The Meters. The Rebirth Brass Band. The Mardi Gras Indians. It's Iko Iko. It's Jazz Fest. It's my friend Tina dancing with an

to realizing it, and has the foresight to bring an extra string of white lights in case the lights decorating the base of your urn burn out halfway through the ceremony.

Your Celebration Master is like a school principal—she won't teach the classes, but she'll make sure everyone does their jobs. She also won't let anyone stray from (or interfere with) your funeral dreams. As head of your funeral posse, your CM will be

---

umbrella in the mud at Jazz Fest. ('Cause, hey, sometimes it rains at Jazz Fest, and it's muddy, but whatcha gonna do?) It's the beat that's all around you in New Orleans. That's what I want to share with my loved ones.

LOCATION: I live in a suburb of San Francisco, which is just not that funky. If we did my second-line funeral here, it just wouldn't be the same. The magic of the second line is about being in New Orleans. To make sure it happens in New Orleans, I'll have to start a fund to fly about 20 friends and relatives there. Better start now.

PLAN B: If it's too inconvenient for my survivors to have my funeral in New Orleans, I'd settle for a big beach party funeral in San Francisco. Maybe a small private church service for the family, then meet up with all my friends from over the years at Ocean Beach or Muir Beach. Invite *everybody*. Have a big ol' bonfire. Barbecue some oysters. Hang out and party. Now that's a party I'd *love* to attend. Can some people bring guitars, please?

responsible for calling the first team meeting, keeping your end-of-life plans on track, and managing the other team members.

I've already recruited two friends from my inner circle, Emily and Katherine, to serve as co-CMs. (I also have a backup CM, Kate, who's half my age; she can take charge if I outlive my current team members.) My CMs will make sure my Food Concierge gets the brownies I like. They'll make sure my DJ plays all of my playlists in the right order. They'll make sure there's a bouncer outside all of my funeral events to keep out the uninvited. And, if I die suddenly and the person in charge of my funeral T-shirts happens to be bicycling through France, they won't freak out. They'll just recruit a few friends to stay up all night before the funeral, silkscreening the T-shirts themselves.

The Event Planner: Choreographer and Merrymaker

Think of your Event Planner as a slightly mad pastry chef who wants to make you a magnificent multi-tiered cake. Obstacles schmobstacles. Nothing will get in her way; no detail will be too small to consider. If she has to fly to Madagascar for the perfect vanilla bean, so be it. And no way will she buckle under time and budget constraints and order a keg for your party because it's easier and cheaper. She'll order the Tanqueray, budget or no budget, because that's the kind of woman she is.

Don't consider anyone for this job who displays even the slightest hint of wishy-washiness. Best to concentrate on your more obsessive-compulsive friends. Even better if they work in the arts so they can help with lighting, staging, choreography, and, if necessary, costumes. You need an Event Planner who can make your vision come to life.

The Memory Maven: Publicity with Panache

Your Memory Maven (or Memory Mister, as the case may be) will set the tone and promote a consistent image of you and your funeral events in the hours and days following your demise. It's best to recruit someone who shares your sense of style and who understands the subtle, yet important, distinctions that make Bodoni a much better choice for an invitation font than Times Roman. How close you are to this person is less important than having invitations that dazzle and entice.

Unless you have a friend with marketing or public relations experience to fill this role, make sure you leave your MM a list of approved designers, writers, producers, web masters, and print-ers. You want professionals creating your invitations, writing your obituary, and directing and filming your funeral video. This is no job for amateurs who *think* they know how to use Photoshop.

I've appointed two people to serve as co-MMs: my friends Kamie and Cornelia, who will take my vision and run with it. They'll produce the death announcement cards and invitations that will have people dying to get on my guest list.

Your Notification Master: Dialing with Decorum

Once your immediate family and closest friends know you're gone, it's your Notification Master's job to get on the phone and spread the word to the rest of your inner circle.

Naturally, you'll want a caring, responsible person serving as your NM. I recommend choosing a close friend to save your family the anguish of repeatedly discussing your demise. A friend might also know more of your friends and colleagues than your family does. Your NM and List Master, who's in charge of main-taining the guests lists for your various celebration events, will work together to inform your survivors about all of your impor-tant post-life functions. If you're keeping your team lean, you can assign both positions to one person.

My LM, Jon, is perfect for both jobs. He has the grace to gently break bad news and the patience to track down anyone on my list who might be hard to find.

Your Family Liaison: The Ultimate Gatekeeper

You'll also need to recruit a Family Liaison, someone diplomatic and kind yet firm, who will be responsible for managing your family through this crisis. Most important, if you're unlucky enough to die young, your Family Liaison is going to have to tell your mother that she's not part of the posse. Nothing against mothers, but if you have a specific life celebration in mind, nine times out of ten you're best off having friends carry out your wishes. Your team can find a way to honor and include your parents in the party of your life and other funeral events that won't interfere with your plans.

Your Body Boss: Getting You from A to B

Last, but not least, you'll need an undertaker, or, if you prefer, a Body Boss—someone who will be your body's advocate and guardian, making sure you make it to all of your appointments, from the time you die until you arrive at your final resting place. You want a friend who has no trouble asserting her (your) wishes, even if it upsets a few people.

As you travel from the hospital to the funeral home (or back to your house, if you choose to have a home funeral), so many people can make mistakes with your body, especially if you die tragically as a homicide victim and end up in the morgue. You need someone looking out for you, or you could end up with bad hair, bad makeup, in a casket (when you'd prefer an urn), or in an urn (when you'd prefer a casket). People make mistakes, especially with dead people, and sometimes people cross the line—especially if you're famous by the time you die.

Someone, perhaps a CIA operative, took the "liberty" of clipping a lock of Che Geuvara's hair after his death in 1967. Who knows where's it's been for the past 30 years, but in 2007, a Texas bookstore owner bought the hair for $100,000. Fair enough if the money went to the cause, but I doubt it. And I doubt Che was in on it. Without a Body Boss, sleazy opportunists may try to profit from your death, or worse, as in the sad case of Napoleon, steal your most private parts.

As the story goes . . . the priest who was supposed to administer last rights slipped a scalpel out of his sleeve and separated

Napoleon from his member. In 1927, the little general wound up on display in the Museum of French Art in New York. In 2007, it made the news again when its most recent owner, a Columbia University professor and urologist, died. (It's unknown whether Napoleon's bone apart will be willed to a museum or relative, or finally be freed to join the rest of his remains in Paris.) Don't let this happen to you; have a Body Boss with you at all times.

Even if you don't inspire any creeps to take samples of you, your grandmother's ruby ring and your fancy Swiss watch might be pretty tempting. Wouldn't you like those items returned to your loved ones? They might not be if there's nobody there to ask for them.

The B Team

Since I could outlive my team members, I've recruited several of their children to serve on my backup funeral team. My youngest team member is 10, and my CM-in-training is 15. They've been briefed, we've agreed to keep in touch for the rest of our lives, and they're fully on board with my fantastic funeral vision.

Don't be afraid to invite your young friends and relatives to serve on your team. They'll probably feel honored to be included. Kids understand and appreciate out-of-the-box thinking, and they love parties.

Your B Team could also include neighbors or other acquaintances who might be willing to step up when it's your time to step down. You never know until you ask.

Going Solo

Finally, if you're still uneasy about the team concept, maybe it's worth taking some time to reflect on why you think you don't have friends who can help you. No man is an island. It's time you reached out to loved ones and renewed your connections. I'm sure they'll be happy to hear from you.

If you still don't think you can pull together a funeral team, it's okay. Selecting a team and making to-do lists for each member are fun exercises for obsessive people like me, but you can have a funeral without a team if you want to. Just get your wishes down on paper and leave a copy with someone you trust. Then that person can recruit (or hire) help when the time comes.

Start Planning Now

Who could keep a team of kindergartners on their toes with a snap of her fingers? Who will remember to use the purple glitter? Who has an inner undertaker just dying to come out?

- Recruit your funeral posse or a single celebration advocate.

- Assign each member a position and duties.

- Assign understudies for each team member.

- Make a list of party and end-of-life professionals who can assist your team.

- Give copies of this information to your team members.

- Store information in your funeral box.

(Note: feel free to adapt, expand, or rename the names of your team members, as well as their duties, to fit your individual needs.)

"I can't think of a more wonderful thanksgiving for the life I have had than that everyone should be jolly at my funeral."

—ADMIRAL (LORD) LOUIS MOUNTBATTEN (1900–1979), British naval officer and last viceroy of India

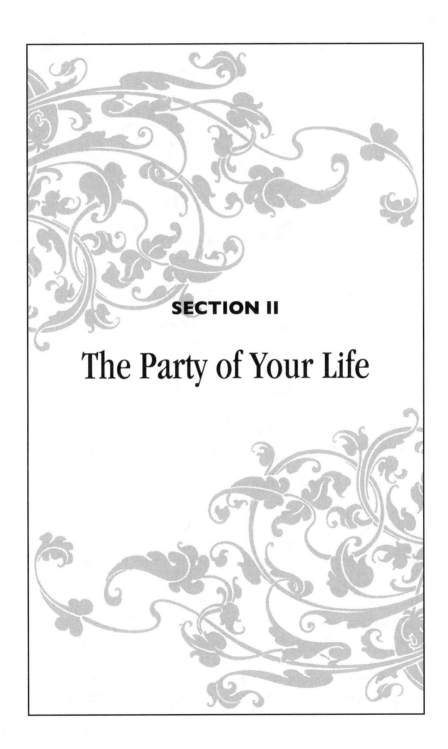

SECTION II

The Party of Your Life

CHAPTER 3

It's My Party, and I'll Die If I Want To

Themes and Dreams

*W*hether your dream farewell is a small gathering of close friends at your favorite wildlife preserve or a weekend-long, booze-filled funeralpalooza for the masses, you need to start planning now to get the funeral you want and deserve.

Share the Fun

*H*ave you ever noticed that the letters in "funeral" can be rearranged to spell "real fun"? I don't think that's a coincidence. It's a message. It's also an excellent starting point for your planning. What's fun to you? What would be fun for your guests?

Make a list of your favorite things, including activities you and your friends have enjoyed together. Don't hold back on any whimsical details; let your imagination run wild with colors, textures, sounds, images, and tastes from your life. Red corduroy pants, Persian rugs, ballroom dancing, knitting, fresh-baked chocolate chip oatmeal cookies, hiking through alpine meadows, veggie pakoras, riding a unicycle, Japanese gardens, drinking gin, foraging for wild mushrooms, kayaking, muffin tops, dharma talks. Feel free to include activities you've only dreamed about or watched from the sidelines—whatever makes you happy. Don't worry about the details; you can always figure out accessibility, seating, and lighting issues later.

The purpose of this list is to get you thinking about what type of farewell you'd like to have. It's not so much about the specific activities you enjoy, or even including them in your funeral lineup (although you certainly have that option) but identifying what makes you *you* and how you might like to be remembered. These ideas will help you develop an overall concept and theme for the party of your life. (You'll read more about planning the funeral service portion of your life celebration[s], if you choose to have one, in Chapter 13.)

Thinking about funerals you've attended will also help you clarify what you want (and don't want). Which ceremonies entertained and inspired you? Who had the best food? Which funerals could have been better if they'd been self-planned?

The More You, the Better

Naturally, your funeral events should be all about you. Don't be shy about infusing every aspect of your farewell fiesta with your interests and passions. There's no reason your obsession with sudoku has to die with you. Or your fascination with Krav Maga. Share as much of your life with your survivors as you want. They'll love the personal touches because they love you.

Any event, or events, showcasing your wit, charm, and talents will comfort and thrill your guests because they'll feel surrounded by you and reminded of all of the good times you've shared. When they find the safety goggles enclosed with their funeral invitation packet and notice the archery demonstration listed in the schedule of events for your funeral picnic, they'll think to themselves, "That's so you."

They'll also think of themselves because they probably still have copies of the safety manuals you've written throughout the years for your birthday parties, as well as the dozens of manuals you thoughtfully created for their baby showers, weddings, and anniversary dinners. Don't forget; your past is also their past. (My funeral rule of thumb: the more *you*, the more *them*, the more they pay attention. In other words, the more you pack your party with elements that remind your guests of the past they shared with you, the more involved they'll feel.)

Your guests will also be grateful for some fresh material. By the time you die, your guests may have attended dozens of funerals. If you want your life celebration to stand out from the others, you need to make it memorable. You can bet that the Massachusetts man who had an ice cream truck at his funeral will be remembered by his guests for a long time.

Your funeral doesn't have to be grandiose, just original. Just all about you.

Dream Themes

Once you have a working "fun" list, make a list of activities and observances you *don't* want in the lineup. That way, everyone will know the boundaries and it will be harder for a meddling relative to dominate the party of your life with his misguided ideas of what's real fun.

Comparing your two lists will also help you clarify a ceremonial style. You'll notice that certain themes and patterns stand out: your love of nature; your fondness for chai lattes; your claustrophobia; your aversion to bagpipes. That's a start—an outdoor fête, a funeral beverage, a disposal preference (cremation), and a ban on bladder instruments. You're halfway there!

You may want to organize the event(s) around a central theme or take a more free-form approach, using random styles, sounds, and images. Both methods have their benefits. Sticking to a specific theme gives your event an elegance and cohesion that your guests will appreciate. It's also enjoyable for you if you have the time. What could be more fun than coordinating color schemes, selecting a funeral font, and working with a designer to create your funeral logo? You don't have to go all Martha Stewart; just stay on theme. Your funeral should be well-planned, but not too slick.

On the other hand, a looser concept may allow you more freedom in packing your funeral and related events with your personal interests. You could have a reggae wake, a *Lord of the Rings*-themed funeral pilgrimage, and a Bowie burial. With your vision and your funeral team's hard work, you can find ways to make seemingly incongruous elements work together to captivate and invigorate your guests.

Write down your ideas now. The more detailed plans you can leave for your survivors, the less time they waste wondering what to do, and the less chance there is that someone will screw up your perfect funeral. Of course, if you can't pull together a crack funeral team or afford a professional to carry out your wishes, keep it simple.

An Arty Party

If you need help getting party ideas, look to the arts. What would Picasso do? Martha Graham? Leonard Bernstein? The party of your life might be just a PBS special away.

Who wouldn't want a Jane Austen funeral? Your guests would be hooked from the start with a flurry of hand-delivered messages leading up to the event. The costumes would be fun to wear. Your athletic friends will have a chance to channel their grief into the thrill of the chase at your funeral fox (or treasure) hunt. Your infirm guests can stay inside for charades, word games, and cards.

In lieu of a wake, throw a dinner party featuring roasted meats, French pottage, fine ales and bitters, and a "to-die-for" cheese platter, followed by a formal ball. Guests young and old will love learning the English country dances they've seen in *Pride and Prejudice*, such as "A Trip to Highgate" and "The Touchstone," as well as "Jacob Hall's Jig" from *Emma*. You'll find instructions and music for a variety of steps in John Playford's *The English Dancing Master* (published in 1651). Visit www.thepartyofyourlife.com for links to online copies of the book and sheet music from the

---

THE PARTY *of* ANN FRANCES WOOLLIAMS'S LIFE

ANN WOOLLIAMS
1956–
Rotorua, New Zealand

SERVICE: A religious service, Presbyterian. I want a hymn that the audience can sing, "How Great Thou Art," and a song to liven it up, "Always Look on the Bright Side of Life" by Monty Python. Then I'd like something quirky, like "Listen to the Rhythm of the Falling Rain," by Donovan. I can only imagine what a group of people singing *that* sounds like.

ATTIRE: All the women are to wear black and go commando. Black hats are mandatory. Veils optional.

SOUNDTRACK: I'd like a solitary Scotsman playing the bagpipes: "Bonnie Banks O' Loch Lomond" as my entrance song and "Amazing Grace" as my exit song.

Jane Austen Center website.

If you die under suspicious circumstances, your team could plan an Agatha Christie "whodunit" mystery weekend full of intrigue and scandal. A Brontë-themed funeral could be the perfect setting for your brooding guests to spend hours walking through the moors, mourning their loss of you. How about a funeral labyrinth?

PHOTOS: There must be photos. This is the only time most family members come together, so each family must get a family portrait.

DISPOSAL: Green burial on a hillside at Kauae Cemetery in Rotorua. It was originally a Maori tribal Ngati Whakaue burial ground. Each guest must make the following toast—"To life and unending joy," with a small thimble of Drambuie. Black umbrellas likely.

FOOD: There must be date scones, pikelets with strawberry jam and cream, little butterfly sponge cakes, tiny salmon and cucumber sandwiches, and cups of tea.

DRINK: Vodka "rainbow" shooters, a drink I invented yet never had the time to patent. Recipe: Line up eight shot glasses. Fill each with 42Below vodka (an award-winning New Zealand vodka). Top off each with a different drop of a colored alcohol (e.g. crème de menthe, Midori, Blue Curaçao etc...). Now you have a rainbow.

Don't have the budget to lease a country manor for your Brit-lit bash? No problem, you can rent out the local VFW and hire a few set designers from your local university to transform the place into an English parlor or ballroom. Dream big, but always be resourceful.

I Love a Parade

As you consider possible party themes, take the time to research funeral customs from other communities and religions around the world. You never know where you'll discover a ritual that suits your creative and spiritual needs.

You might find some exotic ideas just a few states away. Nobody says you have to live in New Orleans to have a jazz funeral. I don't like jazz, but I love the idea of incorporating a parade into my funeral festivities. Processionals have always been a popular funeral activity, not to mention a wonderful show of pageantry and intensity. Who knows, your farewell march could end up on the evening news (if it does, make sure your Web Master gets a copy and uploads it to your funeral website).

A funeral parade is also a bonus for your guests. Nobody wants to sit for long in a stuffy church or funeral home chapel (they won't have to if you plan ahead and select a more comfortable venue). People want to move around, talk, and feel productive. A parade gives your guests the chance to mingle with each other and to stretch their legs (which they'll need to do in order to get limbered up for the funeral disco that evening). It's also the perfect funeral activity for fifth- and sixth-tier friends, children, and the general public, who weren't invited to the main event to participate in your life celebration and honor your memory. Participants can wear Mardi Gras beads with pendants bearing your funeral logo on one side and your photo on the other side. (See Chapter 4 for more ways to add movement to the festivities.)

Real Fun = Big News

Check the newspaper and scan the internet for more funeral ideas and inspiration. You don't want to plagiarize someone else's funeral, but rather find out what's been done and which elements from other life celebrations might help you fulfill your funeral vision. You can always add your own spin on a festive idea, not to mention learn more about your farewell options.

Jade Goody, an English television personality who gained fame and some notoriety during her participation on the British reality show *Big Brother*, is a perfect example of someone who took death by the horns and made it work for her.

Diagnosed with cervical cancer at the tender age of 27, she chose not to mope about her situation but spent her final weeks taking care of business. She married her boyfriend. She made plans for her young children to be taken care of during her funeral. She compiled her funeral song list, including "She Loves You" (the Beatles), "I Don't Wanna Miss a Thing" (Aerosmith), and "Ooh Child" (the Five Stairsteps). Then she orchestrated an extravagant self-tribute that included a vintage Rolls-Royce hearse for her and a 20-car funeral cortège for her fans, featuring vibrant floral wreaths bearing her favorite words and sayings (including several of her infamous public gaffes). A white dove was released during the cortège, which made a stop at her childhood home.

Three hundred invited guests attended Ms. Goody's ceremony, thousands lined the streets for the cortège, and 2,000 well-wishers watched the event on two large-screen televisions posted on the roadside. Her fans rushed music stores for copies of "Ooh Child" in the days following her funeral. I'd say she got the funeral she wanted and deserved.

Not that it's a competition—your funeral doesn't have to make it into the news—but why not consider the media potential of an event all about you? Real fun can also be newsworthy. Your survivors will enjoy reading about you (and about themselves) and your fabulous funeral, and they can save the clippings in the funeral scrapbooks they'll receive at your party. Your nemesis, as well as the general public, fifth-tier friends, and other uninvitees, will read about your funeral with envy and regret, and, finally, since they won't be able to help feeling sorry for you because you died, will still think a few nice thoughts about you.

Who knows, maybe your funeral could inspire someone else to plan a spectacular send-off.

Start Planning Now

How are you going to put the "F-U-N" back in funeral?

- Describe the number and types of celebratory and ceremonial events you'd like to have.

- Make a list of your favorite party activities.

- Consider possible themes and concepts.

- Create an "I don't want" list of any activities or observances you don't want included in the festivities.

- Describe the colors, costumes, and other details of the party of your life.

- Store information in your funeral box.

CHAPTER 4

C'mon Baby, Light My Pyre

Riveting Remembrance Rituals

You can't have a good funeral without rituals. A stellar celebration concept will get your guests in the door, and the promise of funeral gift bags will keep them there until the main event ends. But it's the sacred observances that give meaning to the party of your life.

Distract and Honor

Throughout history, cultures around the world have participated in funeral rites to honor the dead, ward off evil spirits, attract helpful spirits, and prepare the deceased for the afterlife. Rituals also benefit guests by giving them a codified, formal routine to follow at a time when their emotions are completely maxed out. The sounds and smells of a funeral engage the senses, and the small acts of chanting or walking in a procession help each guest connect with your one-of-a-kind funeral energy.

The best thing about rituals: even a small, simple observance can pack quite a sacred punch. Your ceremonial rites can be secular or spiritual, or somewhere in between. They can last for minutes or for days. You can use rituals you're familiar with or adapt rites from other faiths and traditions.

Look past your own culture and you'll find that many communities around the world have a lot more fun with death than we do. During the days-long Dia de los Muertos festival in Mexico, mariachi bands play at candlelight graveside vigils, cemeteries are exactly the places for dancing with abandon, and colorful flowers are fashioned into elaborate displays and decorations. They even have skull-shaped candies!

In the name of personalizing your funeral, feel free to employ any customs or activities that have meaning to you or help you most eloquently express your parting message.

Burning For You

Rituals involving fire are always crowd pleasers. Fire is seductive and symbolic. It's purifying and dangerous. There's something in it for everyone.

Just because you're not a practicing Buddhist or Hindu doesn't mean you can't have a funeral pyre—or at least a symbolic pyre. Get cremated, have your team store you in a beautiful urn of your choice, then have a mini-pyre ceremony. When your master of ceremonies bangs the gong, your guests can walk, march, skip, or dance across a field of prairie grass, an alpine meadow, or other natural setting to the pyre.

While your urned self sits on a table near the fire pit, your master of ceremonies can read your favorite poem or lead the group in a brief call-and-response chant. As guests file past your pyre, they can toss in all of your old parking tickets, your diary, the rejection form letters you received from all the publishers who weren't interested in your novel, your novel, your secret eggnog recipe, and anything else to help you lighten your load on your new journey.

Add a self-help element to the pyre walk by having guests write down the fears and bad habits they'd like to overcome. After incinerating your old baggage, they can circle around and make another pass by the fire pit to toss in their issues. So, their problems die with you. If you like, you can be scattered immediately following this ritual at a nearby waterway (or, if you're a committed Hindu and have the funereal funds to fly a few representatives to deposit your ashes in the Ganges, well, go for it). You can also have a scattering or ash burial later in the month if you'll be having a funeral series.

Ocean Sunset

If you have a crack funeral team and a lot of money, go for the ultimate fire and water ritual: a Viking send-off.

What could be a more exciting combination of theater, history, and pyrotechnics? You get to sail off into the sunset, preferably in your own handmade wooden boat (a project you could start working on now), in a blaze of glory. No embalming. No casket. No burial fees. Just a glowing fireball on the horizon and shimmering orange reflections on the water.

The spectacle from the beach will be amazing. As you drift away and eventually sink, your survivors can party on the beach, the children can gather seashells; everyone will be happy and occupied. It's certainly cinematic. Still, it's illegal, and it may not effectively reduce you to ash. Also, I'm not so sure how historically accurate it is. In the Viking world it was more common to dispose of those worthy of a festive farewell by burying them in a boat laden with riches for the afterlife. Often, the graves were lined with stones in lieu of a boat because . . . well, what a waste of an expensive conveyance.

Still, you get the idea. Hang on to the concept, but adapt your floating farewell to a beach near you. For example, ask your kayaking buddies to carry you (i.e., your urned self) into your memorial party in your old kayak.

THE PARTY *of* SHARI ROSE'S LIFE

SHARI ROSE
1966–
Minnesota, USA

EVENTS: No viewing, but multiple celebration events. Somewhere in the schedule people can create and share their artistic expressions of their experience of me (stories, puppets, prints, what have you). Next, a memorial service. Then, a party.

SERVICE: I'd like to borrow some of the structures of a Kundalini yoga class. I would like to open with everyone breathing together for three minutes, then have everybody chant, "*Ong namo guru dev namo*" three times. At some point in the service I would like someone to lead the 11-minute version of the Kirtan Kriya meditation chant. I'd also like everyone to sing "Longtime Sun" three times ("May the longtime sun shine upon you, all love surround you, and the pure light within you, guide your way on"), which may lead into an extended dance version with musician guests playing instruments and other guests shaking shakers and beating on whatever surface they can find. The service will end with everyone chanting, "*Sat nam.*"

SOUNDTRACK: For the party, not the memorial service, I'd like my musician friends to form a band for the occasion and perform the following songs: "Girl from Ipanema"; "To Life, L'Chaim"; "Gonna Get Through This World" by the Klezmatics; "Rhapsody in Blue"; Glen Miller's "In the Mood" and "Stardust"; "Growing Up" and "Wild Billy's Circus Story" by Bruce Springsteen; "Finger Monkey" by Keith Secola; "Lost in the Supermarket" by the Clash; "Sugar Mountain" by Neil Young; "Kiss" by Prince; "Everybody Lies" by Leo Kotke; "Say Hey" by Michael Franti; "American Girl" by Tom Petty; "Down at the Platypussery" and "Monkey Mind Pirates" by my friend Dave DeGennarro; and "Shari's on Her Bike" (the one song that has been written about me) by my friend David Christman.

DISPOSAL: Green burial, but if it's easier for my family, cremation is okay, too. I want my ashes scattered at the Pinehaven golf course in Guilderland, New York; the desert wash behind my parents' house in Tucson; the Lake Superior inlet at Cornucopia, Wisconsin; and the Great Sand Dunes of Colorado. I'd like some of my ashes mixed with my cat Percy's ashes, some with my husband's ashes if he goes first or at the same time, and some with my mom's, too. I leave it to my husband and friends to scatter the rest of the ashes where they want.

FOOD: Potluck—just make sure there's herbal tea, sugar-free dark chocolate, and fresh fruit.

Funeral Fanflare

Who doesn't love a good bonfire? Even a small campfire is always a hit attraction.

Your personal combustion ceremony can celebrate your favorite lifetime experiences, such as summer camp or listening to Cheech and Chong albums (and adopting their "up in smoke" extra-curricular activities), symbolize your post-life vision or fears (i.e., the fiery pits of hell), or serve as a beacon to the living (quit pouting on the sidelines and live your life before you end up dead like me).

The size of the fire is not as important as lighting the fire, giving the fire plenty of time to burn, and taking advantage of the many ritualistic opportunities a waterside blaze provides. Make sure you have skilled fire masters producing this event to maximize your incandescence and ensure your guests' safety.

Your loved ones won't have a minute to worry about their grief if they're carrying torches in a procession leading to the bonfire site. Ratchet up the adrenaline a bit by having a relay torch event, like the Olympic torch lighting ceremony, where your more athletic guests can work together (and against time, weather, and other obstacles you chose) to transport you (your flame) to your death hearth.

Once the fire is sparked, your master of ceremonies can lead your guests in a variety of stimulating observances. Participants can form a circle around the fire for a singing or chanting rite. Naked or costumed guests can dance around the flames. Drumming and strumming are always popular at beach fires.

Whatever you decide to do, check state laws and city ordinances. You don't want the law to show up at 2:00 AM, and have all your hard work go to waste. Don't think the police won't shut down your funeral. While researching this book I came across a news article about a funeral in rural China that was busted by the cops. Five people were arrested for producing stripper funerals (apparently a common practice used to draw crowds to end-of-life parties). A spectacle is always fun, but don't let the drama over-shadow you. It should emanate from you, but never distract the guests or alert the authorities.

Shine a Light On Me

If you're after the symbolism more than the blaze, you can keep it simple. Sometimes a candle is all you can handle. The small act of lighting a taper can be a spiritual gesture. The light from the flame can symbolize purity, create mystery, remind your childhood friends of your pyromaniac past, or serve as a focus point for a group meditation.

You can have a candle table, where guests light a votive (for you) on their way into your service. Throughout the ceremony, more candles can be lit for symbolic purposes or as a transitional activity between acts. Better yet, use sparklers!

Squelching a flame can also be a powerful spiritual gesture if you want it to be. Throw some candles on your funeral cake! Your life partner or Death Buddy can read your last words to your guests, then blow out your candles, giving you both good luck and confirming that, for you, it's really lights-out time.

With the right people advising you and running the show, you can imbue even ordinary objects and gestures with magic and emotion.

Take Me to the River

It's always a good idea to hold at least one of your funeral events on or near water. Water is all about movement and hope and re-birth. Even the smallest stream will sooth and comfort your guests.

After your guests unload your (and their) baggage on the pyre, how about a rejuvenating flower ritual? Have each guest toss a daisy into a small stream or, better yet, off a bridge into a major river to symbolize your sweet, sunny soul (or as a symbolic gesture to calm your "he loves me, he loves me not" obsessiveness that drove them nuts when you were alive). You can use any flower you like. I prefer daisies because they're honest, straightforward, happy little flowers. Increase the interaction by having guests write loving affirmations, words that describe you, or lines of verse on each petal before they toss their flowers.

If you want a more theatrical rite, go out Ophelia-style on the reedy banks of your favorite river. Naturally, you don't want to drown yourself—that would be a mess for your survivors—but instead have your body minders lay you out in a canoe or small boat festooned with flowers and greenery. You're going for a serene "I've accepted my death and now float peacefully to my next life" look, rather than a post-suicidal "lost my mind over a dumb boy" mien. Best-case scenario, your team can float your boat down the river to your plot in a natural burial ground.

Splish, Splash

Don't forget about your funeral bath! Bathing the deceased is a common funeral ritual in Jewish, Muslim, Hindu, and Buddhist traditions. Who wouldn't want one? You get personalized, hands-on attention and your spouse or partner gets a private, loving way to send you on your post-life journey.

If your family isn't the DIY type, they can hire a death midwife to come to your home and care for you. With a change of clothes and clean sheets, you'll be all ready for your home visitation. Your loved ones can decorate your bedroom with your favorite scarves and set up a mini-museum in the living room, showcasing your collections of handmade quilts, vintage watches, and ceramic tea sets.

Back to Basics

To get started creating your own end-of-life rituals, consider a few simple, time-tested customs: use of sound, movement, and color.

Sound

Singing and chanting are excellent observances because they can be spiritual without being religious. So, guests of all faiths can participate and leave the event feeling uplifted.

Wailing and keening are ideal for ramping up the emotion and inciting drama if that's what you're after. (Some guests will love the spectacle; others will feel uncomfortable watching it, which is exactly the result you want. Make sure your funeral videographer gets plenty of reaction shots).

In ancient Greece and Rome, wealthy families hired mourners to sing laments during funeral processions. This tradition was practiced for centuries throughout Europe. Today in Taiwan, hiring monks and nuns to chant or professional mourners to weep at funeral events is still popular. It seems kind of impersonal to me to hire people to do your guests' work, and laments don't sound very festive unless, of course, they're performed with irony and are part of a performance at your service.

Cymbals, bells, flutes, zithers, chimes, and bugles can be used effectively to shepherd spirits or announce the next stage of a ceremony. Drumming is a staple funeral activity in many cultures. It's noisy, it's primal, and it's effective at provoking mob-like behavior, which your skilled officiate will be able to direct into an appropriate activity, such as dancing (see below).

My friends included a call-and-response "oath" in their wedding that involved all of the guests, as well as the wedding party. Everyone loved it. Before you die, come up with some promises or vows that your friends, family, and guests can make to you and to each other, to carry on living with good cheer and even better deeds.

Don't forget that silence is golden. It's certainly another way to go. According to Navajo customs, when you die, your spirit begins a journey to the next world. That spirit can be interrupted and snagged on someone who's not able to keep his emotions under wraps. A skilled officiate will know how to use silence for maximum effect. Some guests will use the time for prayer or reflection, others will wonder if they left their car lights on. Don't you worry about them; you just get your spirit moving where you want it to go.

Movement

Ritualistic dancing always rocks the house. Have your own funeral rave. Ask your funeral choreographer to create a signature funeral line dance for the party of your life.

Adding sound and movement doesn't have to be loud or chaotic. Sometimes there's art and comfort in the form. Several years ago I read about an Oregon woman with a terminal disease who had a polka funeral in her living room with a few friends and family members. Thanks to her state's Death with Dignity law, she was able to plan the last day of her life, attend her home-based funeral, and, a few hours later, depart on her own schedule. Simple, sweet, and, most important, exactly what she wanted.

Update some old funeral traditions by adding life-sized puppets to your funeral parade, as well as specially designed procession flags bearing your funeral logo. Get buried in your own backyard and have your guests throw wildflower confetti at you as you're lowered into your new quarters. Take the funeral procession concept a step further by organizing a memorial road trip. You can also ask your hiking buddies to scatter your ashes on the next peak they summit, or have your cycling crew pull your casket in the cortège to your natural burial site.

Whatever you do, don't have a bird release. Yes, white doves are beautiful and symbolic. However: 1) It's been done and 2) what if a bird of prey swoops in and kills one of the doves? It's happened. Not so pretty anymore, although I kind of like the swift transition from symbolic to literal.

Color

You can also use color to create a mood, make a symbolic statement, and energize your memorial venue (or parade route).

Red is a popular funeral color—it's bright, it's bold, it's the color of blood. The ancient Mayans believed red represented death and rebirth, so they applied cinnabar, a red mineral pigment, to corpses (especially royal corpses) before burial. In Ghana, red, along with black, is a popular color for funeral attire.

In China, red is considered protective (unless you use it the wrong way and create your own bad luck). At wakes, families cover statues of deities in red tissue or cloth to shield them from the coffin. Red is also the color of happiness, so people don't use it in funeral decorations or wear red attire at wakes. They also don't dress corpses in red because everyone knows that a corpse wrapped in red will turn into a ghost.

White is a common funeral color in Hindu and Buddhist traditions. An all-white funeral would look fabulous on a beach.

A few years ago I saw a darling orange funeral invitation. It was very basic, bearing a small picture of the deceased, the date and location of the funeral, and a request that guests wear orange, his favorite color. I didn't know this man, but the invitation was warm and thoughtful and effectively conveyed how much his friends cared about him. More important, it made me want to attend the funeral.

My funeral colors are going to be black and purple. My funeral seamstress is already working on designs for the embroidered silk tunics my funeral team members will be wearing during my service.

Start Planning Now

What's sacred to you? What will make your spirit shimmy? What's the best way to guide your guests through their grief?

- Describe rites and rituals that sound interesting to you.

- Make a list of rites and rituals you don't want included in your funeral events.

- Ask your friends, family, spiritual advisors, and other important people in your life for ideas.

- If you're planning on including fire and water rituals, make sure you or your team takes care of any required permits.

- Store information in your funeral box.

CHAPTER 5

Let Format Follow FUNction

Events and Itineraries

hether you're envisioning a party that includes memorial activities or a service that's more lighthearted
and celebratory (or both), it should be obvious at this
point that a single event probably isn't going to cut it for you.
Having more than one end-of-life function is a great way to get
the funeral you want and deserve.

Brand New Day

While you're brainstorming general themes and concepts for
the party of your life, keep in mind that:

- ✃ You don't have to stick to the traditional funeral
  format (viewing or visitation, service, reception) or
  the typical four- to five-day turnaround.
- ✃ You want to throw a funeral people will be dying
  to attend.

Think outside the box. Model your final party on any type of celebration that resonates with you: a coronation, a swearing-in, a graduation, a bris, a TV game show, a baptism, the county fair, the Olympic Games. Go with whatever inspires you.

If you want to tap into your unique energy and set a more festive tone for your farewell fiesta, weddings and birthday parties are ideal templates for life celebrations. From the first planning stage, there's always a buzz around making the party perfect and pleasing the guest of honor. As the party takes shape, the excitement grows as planners and invitees alike anticipate the colorful

THE PARTY *of* BECKY LORAAS ZRIMSEK'S LIFE

BECKY LORAAS ZRIMSEK
1967–
Minnesota, USA

VIEWS:	For me, funerals are all about the survivors and what they need in order to feel closure. I've definitely been to some funerals that felt really "right" for the deceased, so I'd like something appropriate for my funeral.
FUNERAL:	I'm not interested in a church service, but would rather have a sunset wine and cheese gathering in a beautiful outdoor spot, perhaps in the arboretum at Carleton College, my alma mater (and employer). Definitely low-key lighting, and because I'm an event manager, mosquito repellent should be available, too, and there should be a bathroom close by.

streamers and balloons, the possibility of a host bar, the party games, the dancing, the cake . . .

I prefer reunions and conferences as model funeral formats. They take place over several days, they feature a variety of interesting and enjoyable activities, and they also include time in the itinerary for attendees to rest or socialize outside of the scheduled events. It's up to you. Pack it all into a fun-filled, daylong fête and be on your way, or select a format that allows your team and your guests more time to memorialize you.

READINGS:	I'm not that into poetry but have heard some very moving readings at funerals. Many of them, though, refer to gravesites and coffins and burial, and I'm not planning on any of that. Maybe a Buddhist quote: "There are those who do not realize that one day we all must die. But those who do realize this settle their quarrels." Then some stories and memories (not too many). If my husband Phil is present, he should have our dogs with him.
DISPOSAL:	Cremation, with no direction on where I should end up. Garden, river, cupboard, whatever.
SOUNDTRACK:	*Sunday at the Village Vanguard* by the Bill Evans Trio because Phil and I like to listen to it at the end of our weekends.
ETERNITY:	If there is such a thing as reincarnation, I would like someone at my farewell service to express the hope that my new life will take place somewhere with decent Thai takeout.

A Weekend of Fun

For the most celebration options, I think the party of your life (and related events) should occur on the weekend. Nothing is more depressing and disruptive than a mid-week funeral. Plus, more people will be able to attend a weekend event, especially out-of-town guests, many of whom might be your oldest and dearest friends. Everyone knows the best fares require a Saturday night stay, so you might as well make a full weekend out of it.

A weekend funeral fest gives you the coverage you need and your guests more time to honor you and comfort each other. You can adapt each "traditional" memorial event to fit your celebration style, or create your own remembrance activities and schedules. Why not beef up the weekend itinerary with more observances and diversions? Your guests probably wouldn't mind a little bit more to do and see during the downtime between activities.

If all you offer is the standard Friday night wake and Saturday morning funeral, guests will end up with an afternoon and evening to fill. If you happen to live (and die) in a major city with world-class museums and other attractions, your guests are going to want to check out the town. They'll feel guilty about it, though, and wonder if it's tacky to do anything other than sit around and mourn you. If your end-of-life itinerary includes an arboretum walk or a harbor tour, your guests will love you even more for considering them during your special day.

Modeling the party of your life on a reunion schedule could be the best way to get the coverage and exposure you deserve, as well as make it worth the trip for your guests. (Not that you're not enough of a draw, but it never hurts to sweeten the pot. Someone else might be having a funeral the same weekend as you are. Give your guests plenty of reasons to pick yours.)

Sample Funeral Fests

As you consider your funeral schedule, keep in mind that your guests need to be comforted, distracted, and engaged, but not kept so busy that they become exhausted or lose focus on you.

Here are a few sample schedules:

EAST MEETS DEATH

Friday

1:00–4:00 PM	In-town guests gather to decorate funeral cookies with your personal mandala and assemble your funeral altar.
4:00–6:00 PM	Out-of-town guests arrive. Relaxation Room open. Guests can rest and revive themselves with jasmine tea and almond cookies. Free foot massages.
6:00 PM	Restorative yoga gathering, including simple breathing and meditative exercises. Guests who would like to move and stretch can remain for a simple 30-minute *asana* practice. Lavender-filled eye pillows provided for *sarvasana*.
7:00–9:00 PM	Dinner at your favorite Indian restaurant, followed by a karaoke party at your best friend's home.

Saturday

9:00 AM	Morning yoga practice and sutra discussion.
10:00 AM	Breakfast of yogurt, muesli, fresh fruit, and chai.
11:00 AM	Guests meet to assemble daisy chains and marigold garlands.
1:00–2:00 PM	Free time for napping, mingling, etc. Snacks (*bhel poori,* mango *lassi,* iced green

	tea) available at the Refreshments Tent.
2:00–3:00 PM	Service, including soothing group chants, guided visualizations, and performance involving daisy chains and marigold garlands.
3:00–5:00 PM	Picnic Buffet—veggie *pakoras*, spinach garlic *dhal*, eggplant *bharta*, mango lassi.
5:00–6:00 PM	Free time for napping, meditation, and visiting Memory Tent, featuring your remembrance displays and installations.
6:00 PM	Panel Discussion—"Compassionate Living," followed by Q & A and neti pot demonstration.
7:00-8:00 PM	Bollywood-style dancing class.
8:00 PM–Midnight	Bollywood dance party. Snacks at the Restorative Services Tent.

Sunday

9:00 AM	Morning yoga practice and sutra discussion.
10:00 AM	Breakfast of yogurt, muesli, fresh fruit, and chai.
11:00 AM	Ash scattering ceremony at a sacred body of water. Spiritual guest performs blessings, leads group chants.
11:20 AM	Presentation—"Playful Mindfulness," followed by eulogies.
12:30 PM	Lunch at the Refreshments Tent. Memory Tent open for viewing.
1:00-2:00 PM	Free time for napping, meditation, and visiting Action Tent, where guests can sign petitions and contribute to the Oxfam donation box.
2:00–4:00 PM	Meditative memorial forest walk around three-mile lakeside loop trail.
4:00–4:30 PM	Group photo.
5:00–7:00 PM	Shuttle service to airport.

A GETAWAY GOODBYE

Friday

4:00–6:00 PM — Out-of-town guests arrive. Hired coach transports guests to beachside venue. Hospitality cabana, featuring fried calamari and cold beer.

6:00–8:00 PM — Dinner at the lodge—grilled salmon, roasted red and sweet potatoes with rosemary, and organic greens salad.

8:00–10:00 PM — "Wake Me Up," a multimedia presentation of your life highlights in photos, video, and song.

10:00 PM — Fireworks display (containing some of your ashes) on the beach, followed by howling at the moon.

10:20 PM–Midnight — Story Hour around the fire pit, featuring everyone's favorite "you" story. Sleepytime tea, hot chocolate, and s'mores.

Saturday

9:00–11:00 AM — Breakfast buffet, free time for beachcombing, exploring trails, etc.

Noon — Ash scattering. Death Buddy reads your goodbye letter to guests, eulogies follow.

1:00–2:00 PM — Free time for weeping, sobbing, napping. Snacks available in Refreshments Room.

2:00 PM — Beach competitions—tug of war, sand castle building, three-legged races.

4:00–5:00 PM — Sushi bar, grilled oysters, saketinis.

6:00 PM — Evening water events—sea kayaking and shell collecting.

8:00–9:30 PM — Beachside barbecue.

9:30 PM–1:00 AM — Tiki lamp processional, followed by bonfire and Top 100 Countdown—your favorite songs from birth to death.

Sunday

9:00–11:00 AM   Breakfast buffet.

11:00–1:00 PM   Outdoor Skills demonstrations.

1:00–3:00 PM   Whale watching boat tour.

3:00–4:00 PM   Funeral cupcakes and tea.

4:00–6:00 PM   Open house—guests can write messages in Memory Book, upload digital photos onto the funeral laptop, and participate in brief videotaped funeral interviews that will later appear on your memorial website.

6:00–8:00 PM   Shuttle service to airport.

AN URBAN FAREWELL

Thursday

6:00–8:00 PM   Inner circle in-town survivors use your season tickets to attend your favorite sporting event, a ballet performance, or the symphony. Recharge Room open, featuring Red Bull, coffee, tea, wine, beer, margherita pizza, prosciutto di Parma, and Castelvetrano olives.

Friday

Noon–4:00 PM   Airport shuttle service for out-of-town guests. In-town guests gather at your favorite spa for funeral mani-pedis.

5:00–7:00 PM   Potluck dinner at your neighbor's house. Each guest can bring a funeral dish from a different country.

7:00–8:00 PM   Rituals led by your Wiccan neighbor and her coven.

8:00–11:00 PM	Obituary and Epitaph Contest results. Reading of the best obituaries and epitaphs written by guests (and submitted prior to the event). Winners receive fair trade chocolate bars, movie passes, and stainless steel water bottles.

Saturday

8:00 AM	Early bird 5K memorial run (optional).
9:00 AM	Breakfast.
10:00 AM–1:00 PM	Shuttles to sculpture garden and aquarium.
1:00–2:00 PM	Memorial planting party in your backyard. Readings by first-tier friends, blessing of the earth by Native American shaman, unveiling of memorial bird feeder and bat house.
2:00–3:00 PM	Light snacks provided in Hospitality Room. Memory Room open.
3:30–5:00 PM	Work party—friends gather at your home to haul your old junk to Goodwill.
5:30–7:00 PM	Dinner featuring locally produced wines, meats, produce, and gelato.
7:00–10:00 PM	Scenic coastal, lake, or riverboat tour. Onboard disco and bar, remembrance video screening.

Sunday

8:00 AM	Early-bird lap swim (optional).
9:00 AM	Breakfast
10:00 AM–Noon	Shuttle to Natural History Museum.
Noon–1:30 PM	Picnic, featuring six-foot funeral sandwich and IZZE Sparkling Juice.
1:30–3:00 PM	Shuttles to airport.

The Funeral Series

Another farewell option is the Funeral Series. Depending on your funeral team, guests, and budget, you might want to plan several party-of-your-life events to occur over a period of weeks or months.

The Funeral Series is an ideal approach if you have several groups of survivors living in different parts of the world, if you want to accommodate some of your family's traditions but still personalize your exit, or if you just can't make up your mind. A series gives your guests plenty of time to find the best airfares, shop for funeral outfits, and train for your funeral footrace and javelin toss. Your family gets some grieving space, and your team gets more time to bring your plans to life.

By spacing out your celebratory fêtes over a period of weeks or months, and by hosting them in different locations, you give more people a chance to participate in your death. A few years ago I attended a friend's memorial barbecue; it was the sixth remembrance gathering hosted by various groups of his friends around the country since the original memorial his family held in another state.

Max Out Your Memorial Potential

You never know—your death might take on a life of its own, inspiring all types of remembrance occasions (for all budgets) wherever you have friends and family. Here are just a few examples of how to get the most out of your death:

- In lieu of a wake, kick off your funeral festivities with a themed happy hour featuring your old home videos, amusing "get to know *you*" parlor games, and canapés and cocktails.
- A funeral tea is a lovely way to spend a Sunday afternoon. Include a tea in your weekend fest or use it as an economical way to host memorials in

various cities. Keep it fresh by having a full British tea with scones, cakes, and clotted cream in one location and a more formal Japanese tea ceremony at the next venue.

~ Have a brief secular or spiritual mini-service at your gravesite. Three months later, have a weekend-long memorial featuring a black tie funeral banquet and a formal ball.

~ Include some moonlight merriment for night owls. Leave your psychic's contact information with your funeral team so they can have her on hand to lead the midnight séance.

~ Appease your family with a small, religious funeral service at their church, then have your funeral team throw a memorial poly-party for friends a month later.

~ Keep it simple, save money, and bump up the intimacy quotient by having your end-of-life events, including your death, at home, in the comfort and privacy of your own bed. It's perfectly legal to have your viewing, service, party, and burial where you lived and loved. (See Chapter 21.)

~ Insist on a 30-day mourning period, during which time friends and relatives must visit your altar to see your daily quote and photo (you can have an online altar for out-of-towners). Once this observance ends, have a brief farewell function near your favorite body of water or at your favorite national park.

~ Send your first-tier friends on a Scattergories tour of your favorite European city. Amsterdam would be nice. After a morning of coffee and happy cakes, they can cycle around the city and sprinkle your ashes near historic landmarks such as the Weepers' Tower (Schreierstoren), the Royal Palace (Konin-

klijk Paleis), and the Van Gogh Museum, and finally, toss any remaining crumbs off of the Magere
Bridge.

🔸 If you choose burial—preferably an environmentally-friendly natural burial—don't bum out your
relatives by having them serve as pallbearers. (At
least actress and funny lady Suzanne Pleshette
broke with tradition and had her best girlfriends as
pallbearers.) Hire Chippendale strippers to carry
you to your final resting place. Or have your casket, preferably biodegradable, pulled by a team of
goats. Be original. Shake things up.

There are so many ways you can make your funeral stand
out from the rest. You just need to take the time to plan now.

Start Planning Now

In the end, how many events do you and your survivors
need and deserve?

🔸 Decide how many funeral events you'd like to have.

🔸 Describe in detail the tone, content, and style of each
event.

🔸 Compose a preliminary schedule.

🔸 Store information in your funeral box.

CHAPTER 6

All the World's a Stage

Your Celebration Location

*N*ow that you have an original party theme, inspiring observances, and an exciting remembrance itinerary, where will you showcase the party of your life? Here's a tip: to get the funeral venue you want and deserve, think like a bride!

I Know a Place

Brides know what they want, and they make it happen. They get married on beachside cliffs, in opulent ballrooms, on ferry boats, in college halls, on the manicured lawns and rooftop gardens of world-famous museums, and everywhere in between. Why shouldn't your funeral party be so artful and enticing? You only die once!

Churches and funeral home chapels are fine if they suit your needs, but if you're planning a secular send-off and you'd like a more vibrant venue than your local funeral home, you'll need a party space you can really personalize. Frankly, I find the standard funeral venues very heavy and the seating very uncomfortable. I want my guests to feel at home, not like they're in someone else's solemn space. I want them to be able to make noise, wail, dance, or do whatever my spirit moves them to do. I'd rather host my celebration in a neutral zone and rely on my officiate to set the tone. I don't want my guests wading through that last stiff's energy, or any dogma to be hanging in the air. I also want my team to have the freedom to decorate the room as I see fit.

There are other considerations. What type of setting best reflects my energy and personality? Which auditorium has the best sound system, stage space, and lighting options? Where can I find the largest screen for my memorial DVD viewing? Are the seats padded? Finally, if I can't afford my ideal celebration spot, which rental space has the lowest security deposit?

You'll also want to consider liability and insurance costs. Will your venue allow pyrotechnics? Is your party room equipped to stage the centerpiece of your memorial circus party, the trapeze act? Will there be adequate parking? Will you need a permit to serve alcohol or can you afford to rent a restaurant or bar for an evening? Don't forget to consider other details such as: wheelchair access for older guests, the number and location of electric outlets, and additional parlors for your Relaxation Room, Hospitality Suite, and other installations and attractions.

Thanks for the Memories

Your life might be too big for a mere tabletop remembrance display. I know mine is. I'll never be able to include all of my favorite song lyrics, book excerpts, quotes, readings, photos, and video clips in my service, so why try?

Providing your guests with a Memory Room they can visit at their leisure in between events gives them the time and space they need to linger over the details of your life. Your funeral curator can arrange your room into an interactive remembrance gallery where guests can play your favorite songs on your display iPod, flip through your old scrapbooks, and view your art if you have any to show. Recreate your old rec room by adding a fluffy couch, along with a few of your well-loved blankets. Then your guests can cuddle up together to watch your memory DVD—just like you used to do together on movie night!

Here are a few proposed highlights of my Memory Room:

- A Women's Wall featuring scrolls containing quotes, writings, song lyrics, and more from: Eleanor Roosevelt, Chrissie Hynde, Zora Neale Hurston, Georgia O'Keeffe, Coco Chanel, Indra Devi, and others.
- Audio clips from some of my favorite Democratic convention speeches, including Mario Cuomo in 1984 and Anne Richards in 1988.
- A display of all the birthday and holiday cards I received in my life. (Yes, I still have most of them).
- Video clips from some of my favorite movies and stage performances: *To Kill a Mockingbird*, *Pee-wee's Big Adventure*, *Richard III*, *Jaws*, *Lost in Translation*, and my friends Brian and Megan performing dance scenes from *Trick Boxing*, their award-winning theatrical production.

Your Room Is Ready

If you have the budget, you can't go wrong with a swanky hotel. It's one-stop shopping for you, and it's convenient for guests.

Having all of your guests in the same place will create an atmosphere of intimacy and fellowship that will energize the group and allow individuals to see each other and catch up during "free" periods. It will also be easier for your funeral team to control, er, guide your loved ones through each activity.

Plus, if the party runs late, the police won't show up—and your drunken guests won't be driving home, just shuffling across the hotel to their rooms. Another bonus of an all-in-one venue: by the wee hours, the people from the wedding party in the next ballroom might spill over into your party and who knows what could happen. Who says hook-ups only happen at weddings? (Note to self: add condoms to the funeral gift bags.)

THE PARTY *of* DANA ROURKE'S LIFE

DANA ROURKE
1964–
Illinois, USA

VIEWS: It feels natural to me, but scares me because it is such a lonely thing.

FUNERAL: I don't really feel the need for one. If my family wants to have a party to remember me by, that would be great, but only if it's not formal and wouldn't stress them out. It's just not necessary. I want it to be a time for them to reconnect with family they may not have seen for a while, or to spend time together mourning (which I hope they won't feel the need to do much of at that point).

PARTY: Just good old rock and roll, food that you only eat at parties (because it clogs your arteries and will *kill you*), drinks that will make everyone relaxed (but not sick the next day), and I want people to dance. An outdoor party would

If you live near natural wonders, a mountain lodge or a cluster of beach cottages would be ideal venues, especially if you'd like to offer a slower paced weekend. A short stroll through an alpine meadow or along a windswept beach between activities will provide the serenity your survivors need to start letting go.

---

be great, but since I can't plan when I will die, it might not be very comfortable for the guests.

ATTIRE: Anything that makes my guests feel comfortable and good about themselves.

DISPOSAL: It's my fantasy to be left outside in a forest to die. I'd like to be laid out under a tree, and let nature take it's course. Nature has always comforted me. Maybe it sounds kind of weird, but I have a strong attachment to the outdoors so I feel like it's the right thing to do. After having a nightmare about being cremated alive, that disposal method is just not an option for me!

Since it's illegal to have my body left out in nature, then I would love to be buried under a wise, old tree. I just want to be in the dirt, no casket, let the worms rejoice! The thought of my remains fertilizing something so wonderful leaves me feeling that my life and body wouldn't be wasted.

LEGAL: My husband and I have both agreed to pull the plug for each other.

Everybody's Doing the Locomotion

Make the party of your life stand out from the rest by hosting one of your events on rails or water.

I wouldn't be caught dead on a "murder mystery" dinner train, but I could really get on board with a funeral train. Keep the party rolling by staging your wake, reception, or an all-eulogy dinner party in an old-fashioned dining car or caboose. Give your guests the ride of your life by including a screening of your memorial video. At about $65 a head, the average price of a dinner train ticket, you can entertain 30 special guests for $1,950. That's $50 less than the average price spent on a casket.

Having a farewell fête on a boat or river barge is another way to provide everything your guests will need in one place. Your floating funeral party will present your guests with the best of both celebration worlds: a temperature-controlled indoor environment *and* a chance to stroll onto the deck for a change of scenery.

Whatever type of conveyance you choose, a moving celebration means nobody ducks out early.

Party Out of Bounds

Looking for a venue with built-in atmosphere? You can't beat an al fresco ceremony.

What could be more evocative of the range of funeral emotions than a natural setting? The chirp of a bird or the rustling of prairie grass in the wind will pluck at your guests' heartstrings as directly as the first few organ chords of "Rock of Ages." The readings, the eulogies, and even the music will have just a bit more impact because your loved ones will be surrounded by beauty and life. They'll also be able to breathe clean air, rather than feel hot and dizzy in a stuffy room.

At my friends' wedding, a bald eagle circled the ceremony site just moments before the bride and groom arrived. It was one of those awesome, goosebump moments, and such a good omen.

They've been happily married for 19 years!

The same could happen at your funeral. Your brother could be reading your favorite poem or telling his favorite *you* story when a little chipmunk scurries up, takes a seat near your favorite cousin, and eats a little nut while he observes the function. Just a furry little reminder that a) Mother Nature is paying attention, b) life goes on, and c) there will be a buffet dinner after all the talking.

Outdoor venues are also ideal for parties. Your guests will feel more relaxed in an open space and they'll enjoy exploring the grounds. An outdoor setting will make your party feel special and will be much more affordable than a ballroom at the Four Seasons. Plus, you won't need to decorate. Host your party at an arboretum, botanical garden, berry farm, state park, or cultural heritage center. Check out the rental facilities at historic cemeteries, too. Many offer lectures, outdoor concerts, and other performances, so why not the party of your life?

Wherever you stage your open-air farewell, don't make your guests sit on picnic table benches or those flimsy folding camp chairs; spring for the comfortable wooden Adirondack chairs. You should also plan for the worst weather. A large party tent, or an indoor plan B room could save the day.

Low Budget Bash

If your eyes are bigger than your wallet, there are plenty of budget options. Community centers rent out meeting rooms (check the rules on alcohol—it may be prohibited or your team might need to get a permit to serve it). Fraternal organizations, such as the Elks Club and VFW, also have party facilities. When I realized I didn't have the $50,000 budget I needed to get the 43rd birthday party I wanted and deserved, I had to adjust my venue expectations. For $150, I found a sweet party spot at my neighborhood Masonic lodge. The hall had a large kitchen and plenty of tables where my guests could gather, eat, and talk. Most important, there was a huge dance floor.

If you just can't find what you want in one venue, look into the cost of renting a coach to shuttle your guests to each activity. Another consideration: if, like me, many of your closest friends live in another state, you might want to have the funeral there. It's certainly less of a carbon footprint for a few of your local friends to fly out to your desired funeral location than for 50 people on the other side of the country to fly to you. Now, if you want your body in attendance at your out-of-state funeral, it'll cost as much as five round-trip tickets, or more. That's why it's best to separate your body from your party, which you'll read more about in Chapter 19.

Finally, don't let lack of finances disrupt your planning. If you or your funeral team can't find or afford the perfect venue (although you have all had plenty of time to look), you can always have a pasta dinner memorial at a friend's house. In the end, the spirit of the event is always more important than the details.

Start Planning Now

Give your team direction and your party a home by selecting a celebration location.

- Make a list of your favorite funeral venues.

- Make a list of amenities you need in a party rental space so your survivors know what you want if they can't afford your first choice location.

- Store information in your funeral box.

CHAPTER 7

Dance This Mess Around

Your Funeral Soundtrack

*I*f you want your guests to "praise you like they should," there's no better way to get their attention than through carefully selected funeral songs, or, as I like to call them, "fTunes." The music of the party of your life will be the thread that ties together every aspect of your life and death, so start sampling now.

If Music Be the Food of Love, Play On

Trust Shakespeare. Music is life. Music is love. Music is essential to any good celebration or sacred event. You cannot have a good death or a funtastic funeral without killer fTunes. You'll be gone, but "the beat goes on." Your funeral songs will have a powerful, if not the most powerful, impact on your guests' emotions.

Your fTunes will provide the cues your guests need to cry, to laugh, and to get off their asses and dance. The music of your death is really the music of your life—a showcase of high-impact melodies that will remind your best friends of old times, rally your third- and fourth-tier friends and distant cousins around your funeral theme, and, most important, help all of your guests tap into your you-ness. If your fTunes can "lift them higher than they've ever been lifted before," they will love and miss you even more. And your funeral will rock! Remember, the more *you*, the more *them*, the more they pay attention.

Your passing-away party playlists will help your funeral team set an appropriate tone for each memorial event and activity. Even if music wasn't part of your life, that's no excuse for ignoring this vital celebration element. If you don't think you can deliver, leave the music up to a trusted team member or professional (you'd hire a caterer to get the food right—why not use a DJ to serve up some delectable fTunes?) See Chapter 16 for examples of how to use your fTunes for maximum effect.

The Stairway to Heaven

As Julie Andrews sang in *The Sound of Music*, "Let's start at the very beginning." Which songs pop into your head when you think about your funeral party or memorial service?

Almost everyone I've ever asked this question has been able to name at least three songs they'd like played at their funeral, or at least describe the style of music they want. You probably have a few melodies coming to mind right now.

If you need help finding your funeral sound, use the five song categories below for inspiration:

1. *Songs you can't die without.* This first list is about dramatic impact. It doesn't even have to contain your favorite songs or musical acts—just songs that feel right to you. What message do you want to send through these songs? Which emotions and memories do you want to evoke? Which songs will make your guests smile because they're "so you"?

2. *Songs that make you happy.* Don't hold back or worry about what's cool. If you genuinely love "Have a Holly Jolly Christmas" from *Rudolph the Red-Nosed Reindeer* (who doesn't—I have the original soundtrack), add it to the list. You, or your fTunes pro, can find a place for it in the final lineup. These songs can be played at any funeral event you choose.

3. *Songs you sing out loud.* This list includes songs you clean to (Madonna's *Immaculate Collection*), songs other drivers catch you singing along to in your car at stop signs ("Won't Get Fooled Again," "Brown-Eyed Girl"), songs that transport you back to a specific time in your life or a special event (the drunken college roommate belting out "Thunder Road"), and the ubiquitous dance songs at your favorite parties ("Love Shack," "Hey Ya").

4. *Lloyd Dobler songs.* Any boom box serenades in your past? Add them to the list.

5. *Songs you have a crush on.* Every now and then you can fall hard for a new song—just that song, not even the band. You hear it on your car radio and you're hooked because who doesn't love having a new breakup anthem ("Fidelity") or a new rock-out-in-your-living-room song ("Rock & Roll Queen") just to smell that teen spirit again? Who cares if you discovered the song by watching reruns of *The O.C.*? Nobody needs to know that. Crush songs should be part of your death, even if they weren't in your life for very long.

Get your list and preferences on paper and into your funeral box. It's okay if some songs fall into more than one category. The goal is to create the list. You can specify exactly how and when you want each song used later.

Who Are You?

Singles are perfect for playlists, but what about the long play? The liner notes? The albums that changed your life? There's an fTunes category for them, too! (You might have already compiled this list for a Facebook Note.)

Long before there were mix tapes, there were albums, and each one was a full-on sensory experience. Albums required some commitment and, in return, held the promise of hours, if not years, of pure stereophonic pleasure. Other albums were the background music for milestone events. What was playing when you drank your first beer? Lost your virginity? Went on your first road trip with friends?

I can easily measure out my life in desert island discs (DIDs), which are still in a box in my bedroom closet. I cannot and will not die without *Quadrophenia* (the Who), *Clash on Broadway* (on

---

THE PARTY *of* GREGG TEHENNEPE'S LIFE

GREGG TEHENNEPE
1964–
Maine, USA

VIEWS: I always liked Woody Allen's stand-up line about having a replica of the deceased in potato salad.

EVENT: Being a musician, I've played at such ceremonies. Sometimes you can sing things that cannot be said. I would hope that my picking friends would come and sing and play. Hopefully, I will have also brewed a keg fairly recently, so they can finish that off as well.

my desert island, double- and even triple-CD sets count as one "album"), *Blue Earth* (the Jayhawks), *Reckoning* (R.E.M.), *My Aim Is True* (Elvis Costello), *Let It Be* (the Replacements), *Greetings from Asbury Park, N.J.* (Springsteen), *Mirror Moves* (Psychedelic Furs), *Special Beat Service* (the Beat), and the Pretenders' eponymous first album. (Note: your "albums of your life" list probably subsumes your favorite bands list, but if not, you can adjust your lists accordingly.)

The best thing about your DIDs list is that it's all about your life. Who your favorite bands were says a lot about who you were. DIDs are ideal for laid-back, all-day outdoor memorial parties, pre-funeral work parties (there's your biodegradable casket to decorate, the gift bags to be filled, the funeral cupcakes to frost, etc.), and special funeral attractions such as your Memory Room or Hospitality Suite. In my case, my DIDs also constitute my "master list," the music I plan to die to if I end up in hospice care or perishing at home from a prolonged illness.

In the bummer case that you die before your parents and friends, your DIDs list will comfort all in attendance because an hour of one of your favorite albums will provide your guests with a more consistent sound than a mixed playlist that twists and turns with each new song. For the first time in their lives, your parents will enjoy hearing your music because it will remind them of you. Your friends will love your music because it was also their music.

Let's Dance

You can't have a good funeral without a "last waltz." Your loved ones need a chance to shake their tail feathers and let go of some serious sorrow.

My death disco will be so easy. Anything that's fast and loud and from the '70s and '80s will work just fine. Abba, the Pet Shop Boys, the Jam, the Go Go's, the Cure, Haircut 100, Cheap Trick. (In fact, how can I not have an entire Cheap Trick-themed farewell event called "Heaven Tonight"?) Of course, I'll slip in a few ballads, because how can there be any funeral hookups without a few slow dances? (Yes, I want people to make out at my funeral!) "Loving, Touching, Squeezing" comes to mind, "Beth" is essential, and Frampton will definitely come alive at my death dance-o-rama. I want my last dance to be the culmination of every homecoming dance, prom, and great party I ever attended. Budget permitting, ladies will be provided with wrist corsages.

Do You Know the Way to San Jose?

Now that you've gotten your Ya-Yas out, you can focus on the more intricate task of compiling a nuanced collection of songs that will beguile and impress your guests at your more sedate funeral events. These fTunes should separate you from the insipid Top 40 crowd and demonstrate your eclectic, sophisticated tastes, as well as provide the backdrop for funeral events where the emphasis is less on formal ceremony and presentation and more on mingling, talking, lounging, or viewing memorial installations.

Your backdrop list can be used for wakes, cocktail hours, and other low-key events where a stellar soundtrack is essential but you don't want anything too loud or up-tempo. You're going for smooth, soulful, jazzy, punchy, boppy, slow, sexy, salty, breezy, and bittersweet. The arrangement itself should have its own rhythm and pace. (You will probably need help with this task. Not everyone has the skills to pull off the perfect party playlist.) You want music that will catch your guests' attention every now and then but not distract them from talking about you. B-sides, cover songs, and old 45s (and 78s) are all excellent places to look for material.

Keep it fresh with a few catchy songs by Jem, uplifting melodies by Yael Naim and Sondre Lerche, and swingin' soul-jazz-folk stylings by Adele. Seventies standards by Carly Simon and Dionne Warwick are always appropriate. You can't go wrong with Elvis Costello or Chrissie Hynde singing Burt Bacharach.

What's fun about this playlist are the little surprises you can throw in to catch your friends off guard. They already know you loved the Who. They attended the concerts with you in '75, in '82, and again in 2006. What they might not have seen is the YouTube video of Bettye LaVette covering "Love Reign O'er Me" at the 2008 Kennedy Center Awards. That will blow their minds. What they might not know is that you like "It's Oh So Quiet," Bjork's cover of "Blow a Fuse" (and, for that matter, Betty Hutton singing "Blow a Fuse"). What they might really enjoy is hearing Bowie sung in Portuguese (Seu Jorge) or a ukulele-strummin' version of "Psycho Killer" (Victoria Vox). Giving your guests new ways to love old songs shows them how much you care.

(Note: if you were a Deadhead, you might want to skip this list and just keep on truckin' with a continuous loop of Dead tunes. Or the same tune. Would anyone even notice?)

Talkin' 'Bout My Generation

Of course, I've been talking about my music. It's only rock and roll, but I like it. If it's not your thing, go with jazz, or klezmer, or techno. You can't go wrong with classical. As my musician friend, Jeffrey, says, "Nothing says death and resurrection like Bach."

Whatever you do, be original. "My Way" tops the charts for UK funerals, but why include a song that's been done by everyone else? "I Will Always Love You" was a popular exit song for a while. But do you really want to depart to that drivel? Let that sticky sap stay stuck in the early '90s. You deserve better. "American Pie" is so milquetoast at this point; it would be sort of pathetic to include in your funeral. Still, it's your day, your way.

If music just isn't your thing and you can't come up with decent playlists, at least think of some ways to make the standard hymns more interesting. Have a friend play them on her fiddle. Stir it up with a sitar band. Feature some funeral folk songs from around the world.

You Are the Soundtrack of My Life

Finally, you might want to think about assembling your funeral
soundtrack, a compilation of songs that would accompany a
movie about your life.

To get started, think of some of your favorite movie
soundtracks and Broadway musicals and what makes them stand
out from the rest. Do they remind you of your favorite scenes? Are
they entertaining in their own right? A stellar soundtrack might
feature a single musical act, such as Simon and Garfunkel in *The
Graduate* or Cat Stevens in *Harold and Maude,* or provide you
with a lineup of songs that will help you relive the excitement
of a live performance, such as *The Music Man* or *West Side Story.*
Other notable soundtracks include compilations of songs you like
but would not have thought to put together, or introduce you to
musical acts you haven't heard before, such as Phoenix in *Lost in
Translation* and Burning Sensations in *Repo Man.*

That's why I love Wes Anderson movies, especially *Rush-
more.* I get to hear the Who, the Kinks, Cat Stevens, the Faces,
and John Lennon, all in one soundtrack. Of course, I have a crate
of Who and Kinks albums in my closet, but I wouldn't buy a Faces album just for "Ooh La La." Same with *Garden State.* I couldn't
listen to an entire Shins album, but a few of their songs sprinkled
throughout a playlist provide the requisite easy-listening balance
I need to create a textured soundtrack.

Because I see my life in cinematic terms, I've already compiled my funeral soundtrack. (I've also left a short list of actresses
who would be acceptable to play me if someone ever makes a
movie about me.) Some songs from this playlist may be used at
one or more of my funeral events; many will not be. This fTunes
playlist doesn't even contain all of my favorite songs, but it does
conjure up a super cool energy and hipness that is my trademark.

My funeral soundtrack is also the last mixed tape of my life
and my parting gift to my loved ones. (If you were born in the
'80s, or don't understand the importance of mixed tapes, watch

High Fidelity ASAP.) Naturally, I've left instructions for my funeral team to distribute iTunes gift cards in my guests' gift bags so that all of my loved ones can download my funeral iMix. What's so awesome about my funeral soundtrack is that my first- and second-tier friends will totally get it, but because it's so well done, most of my other guests will also get it for totally different reasons. They'll get that feeling that my funeral soundtrack isn't really about my funeral. And it's not. "It's my life . . . don't you forget."

Start Planning Now

Get out the vinyl, search your car for those lost mixed tapes, scan your iTunes library. Put your death to music while you still can.

- ❧ Make a list of songs you'd like included in your end-of-life events. Feel free to ban songs, too.

- ❧ Compile your playlists (or assign a team member to assemble them, or to hire a professional when the time comes).

- ❧ Specify how you want songs and playlists used.

- ❧ Leave instructions for where your team can find your music—on your hard drive, on your iPod, in a box in your closet, etc.

- ❧ Store information in your funeral box.

CHAPTER 8

There You Go

Your Funeral Mission Statement

*N*ow that you've given some thought to what your funeral will look and sound like, and where it will take place, it's time to develop your funeral mission statement.

Death Direction

Your funeral mission statement will keep you focused and provide your funeral team with a succinct description of your funeral vision if you expire before completing your planning.

Start crafting your mission statement by thinking of key words that describe the event, as well as words that describe how you would like your guests to feel: fanciful, formal, stylish, sad, shimmery, silly, spiky, squishy, sexy, supple, silky, scary, spectacular, sweet, simple, serene, pink, purple, pretty, plump, peculiar, pleasant, happy, hopped up, high, heroic, elegant, elegiac, energized, etc. Then pick a word or two that best describes your ideal funeral. Keep in mind any themes, events, music, and even funeral beverages you've considered up to this point.

Also, remember that your funeral dreams may change as you work through this book and learn more about your options. Your funeral mission statement will probably still work because even if you alter the content and activities of the party of your life, the tone and style of your vision will likely stay the same. If not, you can revise your statement as needed.

Sample Farewells

It may take several attempts before you're able to distill your dream funeral into a coherent statement. In fact, you may need to be further along in your planning to create a funeral mission statement. That's okay; you can always come back to this chapter after nailing down your main concepts.

Try to keep your mission statement to three or four sentences. Here are a few examples of funeral mission statements:

- My goodbye gala will be a whimsical affair, ruled by mirth and frivolity, decorated with silk ribbons and sprigs of fragrant rosemary. Velvet-festooned jesters will entertain each table with magic tricks, bawdy jokes, and tumbling exercises.
- My last luau will commence with a brief surfing exhibition before the sun sets and end with a fire knife dance competition at dawn. Guests will dine on roasted pig, grilled vegetables, and dragon fruit sorbet.
- My noir-ish nod-off begins in a dark alley in Chicago. It's raining. A tall stranger lurks in the shadows, smoking an unfiltered Pall Mall, his face obscured by his fedora. Guests wander toward him, frightened and confused, until they find the secret entrance to the party, held in an abandoned, dirty insurance office. Once inside, they'll be greeted by revelers shaking noisemakers, and peril will quick-

ly transform into party!

 ❦ Lay me to rest in a plain linen shroud at my favorite all-natural green burial ground. No chemicals or caskets or makeup for me, just plant a little sapling that will grow into a tree. Don't pray or sing any ballads, I'd rather you all shared an organic Caprese salad. Take your time and dine, enjoy some fine wine.

 ❦ My life was a cabaret. My funeral will be, too. I want cancan dancing! And singing! And absinthe! And men in drag! Also, I want a man in drag to

---

THE PARTY *of* EMILY STEVENS'S LIFE

EMILY STEVENS
1963–
Minnesota, USA

VIEWS: I hope I'm old enough when I die that not a lot of my peers are able to make it (not because they'll be dead but because we will all be too old to be shocked by any of our deaths), but not so old that I've lost all my marbles and am completely infirm.

PARTY: Small and cheerful. I hope my son will be there with what I assume will be a family unit of some kind. I also want him to have some supportive friends there who will tell him he had a fun mom who had a long life. These plans will evolve over time, particularly the

jump out of a cake while dancing and singing!

If you have trouble writing your statement, or if your death is imminent, trying making a list of the three or four most important elements (examples: your color preferences, your menu ideas, your entertainment choices) you want included in (or to define) your end-of-life events.

Of course, you don't *have* to have a funeral mission statement. It's just a fun exercise. If you're bed-ridden and dying slowly, it's something for you to do with visitors when you run out of things to talk about.

---

musical choices, which are rooted in the early 21st century, but this is good for now.

SOUNDTRACK: This will be entirely up to my son, but what comes to mind as "must-die-to" songs: U2's "Beautiful Day" and Duran Duran's "(Reach Up for the) Sunrise" because they make me feel happy.

DISPOSAL: Cremation. I want my son to scatter me somewhere happy and meaningful—somewhere he and I haven't been yet, or at least haven't identified, but I'll know it when we get there.

ATTIRE: Comfort before fashion, but I do like basic black with a shock of color or some wacky leopard print.

WILL: My son gets it all, of course.

Your Death Tagline

You also don't have to have an event tagline, but why not? Again, it's a creative exercise for you, it will amuse your guests, and it will help your funeral stand out. Your tagline can be an expression of your attitude toward death or, if you want to stay on theme, a catchy statement characterizing your particular exit style. You can print it on your funeral T-shirts and mugs, and include it on the last page of your funeral program, underneath your funeral logo.

Here are a few examples of fun funeral taglines:

- "Had a blast; sorry it didn't last."
- "Time to go; hope you enjoyed the show."
- "I'm dead; put me to bed."

(Note: your tagline is not the same as your epitaph, although you are certainly free to have it inscribed on your urn, mausoleum, or headstone, if you wish.)

Start Planning Now

How do you spell celebration?

- Identify some funeral words and sounds that appeal to you.

- Clarify the three or four elements of your final celebrations you can't die without.

- Write your funeral mission statement.

- Write your death tagline.

- Store information in your funeral box.

"Live your life that the fear of death can never enter your heart. Trouble no one about their religion; respect others in their views, and demand that they respect yours. Love your life, perfect your life, beautify all things in your life. Seek to make your life long and of service to your people. Prepare a noble death song for the day when you go over the great divide."

—CHIEF TECUMSEH (1768–1813),
Shawnee Nation chief

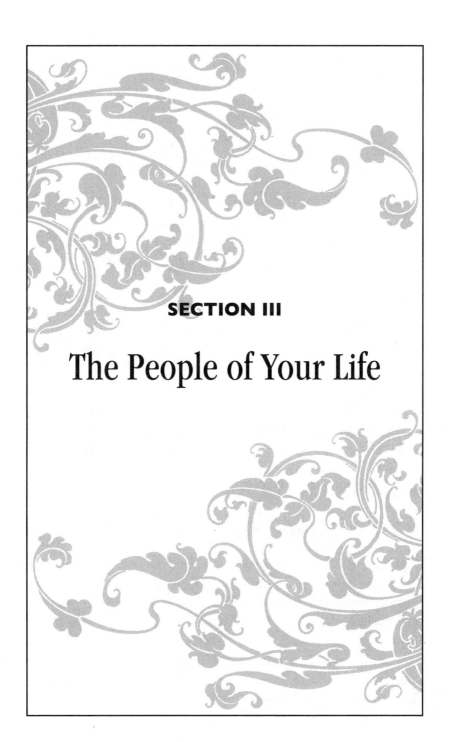

SECTION III

The People of Your Life

CHAPTER 9

Who's Hot, Who's Not

The Guest List

When planning your funeral, it's important to create a detailed guest list. That way, if you expire before reading this book or committing any plans to paper, you can rest in peace knowing that, at the very least, your favorite people will be with you at the end (and your enemies will be stopped at the door if they try to crash the party).

The Invitation-Only Funeral

Perhaps it's never occurred to you that you can invite (or not invite) people to your funeral. That's because, until recently, most people didn't get involved in their own funerals. They just died and left it up to their grief-stricken survivors to throw something together.

If that type of random, last-minute approach is okay with you, fine. But consider for a moment the immediate benefits of the Invitation-Only Funeral:

▪ You get to spend time assembling a list of people you love, like, and admire. What could be more life-affirming than creating a permanent record of all the people who care about you?

▪ You get to fantasize about your guests missing you, talking about you, naming their children after you, and donating memorial benches in your name to local parks.

▪ You get to let your imagination run wild wondering if the celebrities you invite will show up. It could happen. At any time, Harrison Ford or Hugh Jackman or Meryl Streep might be in your town promoting a movie. Maybe Ellen or Oprah will be in your funeral city, taping a special episode. Who's to say that they wouldn't consider stopping by for a drink or two?

▪ Finalizing your list gives you the perfect opportunity to reconnect with old friends. If you haven't had a big party in a long time or just haven't kept in touch with people, you might be surprised by how uplifting and enjoyable it is to recall old times, flip through yearbooks, and pull out old photos. You were cuter than you thought!

Another bonus: now you'll have a complete mailing list to use for holiday cards, press releases, and newsletters, as well as planning parties and reunions, until you die.

Talk of the Town

From a public relations standpoint, the "invitation only" funeral lifts your end-of-life party out of the humdrum community announcement section of your town newspaper and turns it into an exclusive event shrouded in mystery and glamour. By limiting the number of guests to a select list, you'll increase your attendance because, of course, everyone loves to be part of the chosen group (and they'll want to see who else made the cut).

Your invitation-only funeral will also generate curiosity among the uninvited. They'll wonder, "Who's on the guest list? Will there be many famous people there? How can I get in?" Naturally, you want to have a funeral that people are dying to attend. The buzz generated by all the speculation will spill into the funeral and infuse it with just enough drama to keep your guests stimulated and focused. You can't buy that kind of publicity.

The A-List

In the spirit of getting the funeral you want and deserve, feel free to invite anyone you want. This is the only party you'll ever have where you don't have to worry about seating arrangements, or whether your high school friends will get along with your col-

---

THE PARTY *of* KEVIN BRITTEN'S LIFE

KEVIN BRITTEN
1960–
Phnom Penh, Cambodia

PARTY: Everyone is invited. There will be plenty of music, chanting monks (I want nine monks), and then some disco music. Here in Cambodia, they usually have a funeral in front of your home, under a huge awning in the street. There will be lots of booze, and loudspeakers blasting music. I'll need a

lege friends, or if your spouse can handle being in the same room as your ex(es). All conflicts between guests will take a back seat to the collective emotions of grief and nostalgia.

Everyone there will know it's all about you and behave accordingly. In the rare case that a skirmish erupts, you won't be there to worry about your guests feeling uncomfortable. Relax, and let your living worries go. You'll be dead when it all goes down. Your survivors will get through this party just fine.

Selection Criteria

When planning your guest list, you'll need to establish some basic criteria to help you determine who makes the cut. Initially, your decisions may be influenced by what type of funeral you want and by how much funeral you (or your loved ones) can afford. With more thought you'll begin to see the bigger picture. You want an ensemble of friends, relatives, and acquaintances

---

huge awning so there's room to accommodate the coffin and provide enough room for all the guests to kneel and pray and to sit down and eat.

RITUAL: The whole process is repeated 100 days later to make sure that your spirit is really gone.

DISPOSAL: Cremation at the pagoda, then my guests will scatter my ashes in the Mekong River.

FUNERAL TEAM: My staff, my office manager, and my right-hand man will pull together the event. I'll leave the details up to them.

who will honor your memory, grieve their loss of you, and totally notice your good taste in pre-ordering the hand-sewn purple velvet dinner napkins.

I like the idea of casting a wide net, but also following specific guidelines. Obviously, my invitees must love me and remember me as cute, funny, compassionate, brave, smart, stealthy, and nimble. It's a bonus if they all get along, but most important, they must come ready to rock, they must spend at least half an hour in my Memory Room learning or relearning the highlights of my life, and, while dancing to the Clash, they must not be concerned about the security deposit. Top of my list are my best friends, my second-tier friends, some of my third-tier friends, my family, my UPS man, and my third-grade violin teacher (who totally rocks).

In order to fully grieve their loss of you, your guests need to see every area of your life represented—in photos, in the music you select, and in other guests, such as your childhood neighbors and schoolmates. (You want the group to have some texture and variety—not the uniformity of a fraternity reunion). As you review your list of loved ones, don't forget some people with whom you may no longer be in touch, but who were important (or at least regular fixtures) in your life at one time:

- The guy from high school who always rushed the stage at school dances, cigarette lighter blazing, shouting, "Freeeeebird!" He might be a fourth- or even fifth-tier friend (or in a work-release program) at this point in time, but he will definitely keep things lively at the party of your life. (Note: advise your survivors to monitor his gin consumption.)
- Your childhood friends from the old neighborhood. Kick the Can, Truth or Dare, countless acts of neighborhood vandalism. There's a bond there. They should be invited.

&. The Sweet Old Lady who taught you how to read or how to play the piano or how to be a mime. We all have a Sweet Old Lady in our lives, someone who represents the purity, kindness, and patience that we never had. She should be at the party to balance out the energy. (Note: advise your survivors to monitor her gin consumption.)

Thank You for Not Coming

Feel free to leave some names off of your guest list, or to take it a step further and create a "do not invite" list. In fact, if you want and can afford a huge funeral, maybe you don't need an "invite list" at all—just a "do not invite list." Some people may think it's petty to exclude anyone who wants to pay their respects, but they haven't walked in your shoes. They don't know the pain, boredom, anxiety, and irritation that some people from your past have caused you.

I also advise against wasting invitations on people who don't understand your funeral vision or on people you want to make jealous. It's tempting to invite your nemesis so he can see just how many people love you (and, in doing so, realize that his own funeral will be a drab, insipid affair because *you* are more loved than he is because you did your personal work, and, as a result, lived a life full of meaning and promise and worth). Please resist this momentary lapse of judgment. This is not the most effective way to rub your great life in someone's face.

By inviting this bum to your special day, you're showing him that you care about what he thinks or feels. Then he wins, and you're too dead to have the last word. As my good friend (first-tier) Emily once said to me about my nemesis, "Let him wonder." Remember, this is your day. It's not about him; it's about *you*. Trust me, when he arrives uninvited, which he will, and the bouncer scans the list once, then twice, and then, after consulting the Event Planner, looks your nemesis in the eye and says, "I'm sorry, but nobody here knows who you are"—that's when you win.

Making Waves

Having a "do not invite" list isn't just about you; it can also save your loved ones and an ex-spouse from unnecessary stress. Even if you had the most acrimonious divorce possible, your ex may feel obligated to attend your funeral. However, her presence there would actually upset your family and friends. Let your ex off the hook, and let your survivors know that's the way you want it. Same goes for your co-workers.

Some of your colleagues might actually want to attend your funeral; others will feel obligated. An invitation-only funeral helps all of your survivors clarify their roles in memorializing and honoring you. Now your cubicle buddy from work doesn't have to miss his weekend trip to Door County for your funeral when you won't even care if he attends anyway.

It's not selfish or small to keep some things, like your funeral, private. My friend's grandmother was devastated by her husband's funeral. First, her husband's boss (and nemesis) showed up; he'd made her husband's work life a living hell for decades. Then, the boss's wife took over the post-service activities as if she were the host! What was supposed to be an intimate family gathering turned into an office tribute by unwelcome "guests." Don't let this happen to you or to your survivors.

Don't forget to include some celebrities on your "do not invite" list. Your prolonged illness or tragic death might make the news, especially if you're famous by the time you die or a highly visible humanitarian-philanthropist-environmentalist. Then some washed-up singer or game show host decides to call you and wish you well on your deathbed. Undoubtedly, he'll decide to show up at your funeral. Then guess who becomes the center of attention on your big day?

Private Life

If you're worried about offending the uninvited, don't be. Most people will assume that your family, who might not have known to invite them or who decided on a small, private memorial, assembled the guest list. Also, people understand that sometimes guest lists are limited by budget or venue constraints, or by security issues for the attending celebrities. There are other ways the uninvited can honor your memory.

Your guest list rejects can organize a "walk for peace" event in your honor, attend the public unveiling of the sculpture you commissioned for the local park, or contribute to the memorial fund your survivors set up with your favorite charity. Of course, there will be a commemorative bracelet involved with your funeral logo inscribed on the inside, so your uninvitees, and the public at large, can all participate.

The Dance of Death

It's not so much that you're banning people as choreographing an event based on positive, loving energy. As a courtesy to your invited guests, it's only considerate that you protect them from the awkward moments of having to deal with boring people, cranks, or strangers who walk in off the street.

If you're a people pleaser and still feel a bit concerned about the invitation-only concept, think about this: your funeral represents either the end of your long, productive life or your tragic, painful, and untimely death. Either way, you're the one who deserves a break. No one will begrudge you your perfect day. Invite or uninvite exactly whom you want.

The Kids are Alright . . . Or Not?

As an added security measure (as in, securing that your life celebration goes down exactly the way you want it to), consider whether or not children will be welcome at your funeral.

On my special day, some whiny kid isn't going to disrupt the action or dampen the mood with his selfish little drama. My funeral is going to be all about my selfish little drama!

Some people, mostly those with young children, may disagree with me, and that's okay. The thing is, it's not just about the noise and disruption that could bother your other guests. If someone's child isn't old enough to sit through the service you put so much time into planning, then her parents won't be able to focus on you. Then they miss out on a spectacular event and maybe even the chance for real healing to begin.

If you want to risk it, go ahead and allow kids at your funeral, but perhaps you could set age limits. The cut-off age for my funeral is 10. Any children at my funeral must be invited, be able sit still, know how to light their own torches for the midnight bonfire, and appreciate the Indian-Thai fusion buffet at my funeral feast (there will be no kiddie menu).

If you're not comfortable making such boundaries, restrict the little ones to a special room. Request that parents bring their own babysitters or, if you have the budget, provide them yourself. Funeral homes everywhere are adding amenities—such as kids' rooms stocked with toys, a television and DVD player, and other attractions that tiny guests will be dying to play with—to accommodate modern farewells.

Check It Once, Then Twice

As you create your guest list(s), include each potential guest's complete address, phone numbers (work, home, and cell), and email address(es).

You might want to add some background information detailing how you know each person, as well as the length and nature of your relationship (or at least highlight your favorite people with stars, numbers, or some other symbol or ranking system). That way, your funeral team or next-of-kin will have enough information to help them perfect the seating chart for your funeral brunch, propose carpooling connections for your air balloon ash drop, and order memorial coffee mugs for special guests. These little touches will make your funeral stand out from the rest.

Start Planning Now

Don't even pretend you haven't been thinking of a few people you'd like to uninvite to your funeral. While these thoughts are fresh in your mind, take a few minutes to make your wishes known.

- Create your guest list.

- Make a "Do Not Invite" list.

- Describe the age restrictions for your various end-of-life events.

- Make sure your List Master knows where to find your list(s) once you're gone.

- Store information in your funeral box.

CHAPTER 10

Menus, Massage, and Mojitos

Care and Feeding of Guests

*N*aturally, your funeral will be all about you. It should also be all about your guests. They've loved you and taken care of your needs your entire life. Many of them dutifully helped carry out your funeral plans. All of them made an effort to dress up and participate in the party of your life. They deserve some special care and attention.

Nearer My Guide to Thee

Nobody likes showing up at a funeral wondering what to expect. People want to know what the event will entail, what their role will be, and, frankly, what's in it for them. Set the tone right from the start with a preview of coming attractions in your funeral invitation.

Then, use your funeral website to provide more details, such as logistical, travel, and parking information, weather forecasts, menu options, and a list of local accommodations. Of course, you don't want to give away all of your surprises—that would take away from the natural dramatic tension of the day (or weekend)—but your guests will appreciate a little heads-up so they know what to wear, what to pack, how to accessorize, and whether or not there will be low-sodium meals provided.

Older guests can plan around their pill-taking and nap times; guests with children can sign up in advance for the on-site funeral daycare; and your friends will appreciate knowing about Wi-Fi access at your various events. You want to give your loved ones enough general information so they can be adequately dressed and arrive on time but not so much information that they might start wondering if they really want to participate in ritualistic sword play.

As guests arrive, your team can hand out programs detailing the schedule of events, the rules for your funeral orienteering competition, the sing-along lyrics, the protective eyewear for the pyrotechnic portion of the evening, and any other information and items that will help your guests fully participate in the party of your life. With thoughtful preparation, you can calm and engage your guests mind, body, and spirit before the festivities even begin.

Body and Sole

Show your guests you've considered their mourning needs by padding your funeral schedule with a few mini-attractions. All you need is a venue with a few extra rooms and some thoughtful amenities, such as a funeral masseuse.

Most people would never admit it, but one of the reasons they dread funerals (and other parties) is because they don't want to sit or stand for long periods of time. And they don't want to be bored. Your guests will be in enough pain; none of them wants a sore back or swollen feet, no matter how much they love and miss you. In your funeral Relaxation Room, weary guests can refresh and regroup between activities. Some will want to flop into a comfy reclining chair; others may want to meditate. Everyone will want a free 30-minute massage!

Your team can easily set up a room with subdued lighting and sparse but symbolic decorations, such as a bamboo plant or a desktop rock garden, meditation pillows, and some soft ambient music, as well as a separate annex for the treatment room. Guests will be soothed with a tension-relieving neck and head massage, then energized with a brief foot massage.

Your Relaxation Room (or tent, if you have an outdoor funeral) might be more affordable than you think, and your guests will love it. Budget willing, you could hire several massage therapists to host the room. Again, it's about allocation. If you opt for direct cremation over traditional burial, you'll save $1,300 ($2,000, the average amount spent on a casket, minus $700 for low-cost cremation in a cardboard casket, not to mention the thousands you'll save by not purchasing a plot) and can easily afford a Relaxation Room. Four massage therapist for four hours at $60 an hour is $960. That means 32 guests receive a half-hour rub, and you'll still have money left to cover the Dr. Hauschka facial care kits for your funeral team gifts. Sounds like a funeral I'd be dying to attend.

Including a Weeping Room at your funeral is another thoughtful touch. Your guests, especially your most distraught invitees, will appreciate having a private sanctuary where they can weep, sob, and wail until they feel the release they need to rejoin the party. Ask your team to add a Quiet Room, too, where guests can make offerings to your funeral altar and spend time reflecting on their feelings for you. On their way out, they'll receive a funeral fortune cookie containing a motivational affirmation.

Bottom line: the happier your guests are, the less likely they are to duck out early.

Let Them Eat Meat

You might think that you're the main attraction at your end-of-life party, but at a certain point, everyone will be thinking about the food. Whether your funeral feast is purely celebratory or marks the end of an observatory fasting period, your guests will want to nosh before the night's over.

Your vegan friends will wonder if there will be anything there for them to eat. Everyone else will wonder if you'll stick to your vegan principles even in death and, if so, can they slip out unseen for a few minutes to get a burger? Whatever your team serves, make sure they offer several options, as well as appetizers and canapés during the drinks portion of the event, to account for individualized diets and food allergy issues. Most important, make sure there's plenty to go around. It's also a good idea to keep an EpiPen or two on hand as well. You wouldn't want the peanuts

---

THE PARTY *of* BIX SKAHILL'S LIFE

BIX SKAHILL
1965–
Minnesota, USA

DISPOSAL:	I want to be cremated and have my ashes scattered in a casket.
SOUNDTRACK:	I want "Waterloo Sunset" by the Kinks played at my funeral; it always makes me happy when I hear it.
OTHER IDEAS UNDER CONSIDERATION:	I'd like to be buried with a revolver and a copy of e. e. cummings's *Complete Poems.* For the viewing, I want to wear a suit, but be naked from the waist down.

on your pad thai killing off your cousin. Or would you?

Years after you're gone, your guests might not remember what type of flowers were used in the riverside wish-casting petal ceremony, or even your distinctive funeral hand gesture. But they will remember the food. I don't want to put too much pressure on you by saying that a good spread can make or break your funeral fiesta, but food is really a very important part of the event. I attended a fabulous wedding two years ago, and some people are still commenting about how dry the cake was—despite a gourmet dinner featuring locally-grown vegetables and an impressive selection of grilled meats.

Anytime someone mentions the word "funeral" around my friend Mary, she gushes about the shrimp tempura she had at a Southern funeral for one of her relatives (in the South, they take funeral food very seriously) more than 10 years ago. Her descriptions of the crisp, flaky, deep-fried batter and the succulence of the tender sea meat, not to mention the vast array of dishes in the buffet, are so enthusiastic that I can't even remember who died!

What type of food you offer will depend on your tastes and on what you think your guests would like. Do you serve your favorite foods . . . or theirs? Your overall theme might also influence the menu. If you're going to have an "evening in Paris" funeral, serving barbequed chicken wings probably won't fly. Besides, messy finger food isn't fun when you're dressed up (or advised if you allow small children at the event—nobody wants greasy red stains on their black silk dresses and suits).

A sushi bar would be fun, but you'll want to include additional on-theme dishes for people who don't like raw fish. A pan-Asian menu would be colorful and provide your guests with a variety of options: chicken satays, eggplant skewers, papaya salad. Or, keep it simple with a rustic menu of wholesome vegetable soup and big chunks of hearty multi-grain bread for the vegans and a mutton stew for your carnivore guests.

Another option: use your funeral buffet to teach your guests about funeral foods from around the world. Funeral rituals, especially community-wide funeral festivals, always include food. Take a few minutes to do a Google search, and you'll find plenty of menu suggestions. Or, check out the book *Death Warmed Over* for these recipes: Lemons Stuffed with Sardines (Spain), Spicy Pineapple Salad (Indonesia), Funeral Rice (South Africa), and Maori Bread (New Zealand). (Visit www.thepartyofyourlife.com for more funeral-related cookbooks.)

Food = Mood

The easiest way to feed and satisfy your guests is to hire a top-notch caterer who can prepare and serve the food, as well as plan an appropriate menu. If you've already expended your funeral budget on stage lights and the installations in your Memory Room, you can still have a successful funeral banquet. Lack of funds should never stop you from having the party of your life.

For my West Coast and Midwest 40th birthday parties, I had potluck dinners. In both cases, my local birthday team did an excellent job of feeding my guests. In advance of my Midwest event, I simply submitted a list of my favorite organic foods to my dinner concierge, my dear friend Steph. When I arrived at my party, the table was covered in the most delicious vegan dishes, just the way I wanted. For that same party, my pastry chef, my dear friend Lisa, made 40 chocolate cupcakes with chocolate espresso ganache filling and hand-decorated each one with an illustration of my smiling, bespectacled face. My dear friend Jon ate six of them.

If you don't have friends on your team who are willing or able to pull together a funeral feast or sustain a short-term repetitive strain injury creating personalized sweets, there's always the cold salads, deli meats, vegetable trays, and cheese platters at your local supermarket. You can't go wrong with Whole Foods. They have the best deli and take-away food, and they cater parties! If you don't have the budget for such fancy foods, you can always buy in bulk at Costco.

Whatever you serve, use china, silver, and drinking glasses, or compostable plates and cutlery. There's no sense in adding to the landfill by using disposable dinnerware. (Visit www.thepartyofyourlife.com for links to eco-friendly party supplies.)

Sweet Remembrance

Cakes aren't just for birthdays and weddings. They're also a popular funeral food. Throughout history, people have used funeral cakes as offerings to the dead (or to their protective spirits), as gifts for funeral guests, and as festive treats.

According to Hindu tradition, after the cremation of a loved one, families participate in a 10-day funeral ritual that involves placing a sweet cake, called a Puraka Cake, in an altar each day. The cakes represent the body elements the deceased will need for the afterlife, and are disposed of in a sacred body of water after each ritual.

Funeral cakes were especially popular in the Victorian era, although the sweet remembrance has taken many forms—a biscuit here, a cookie there. Back then, when mourning was an art form, grieving families didn't have to worry about creating their own funeral sweets—there were bakeries that specialized in funeral cakes. In Britain, each guest was given an individually wrapped funeral treat. The wrapping was decorated with common memorial icons, such as a heart or cherub, the deceased's name or initials, and sometimes a line of poetry. Dutch funeral cakes were more like shortbread, with writing or images imprinted and baked into the dough. Oddly enough, most of these cakes weren't consumed either. Guests often saved them as cherished mementos.

I think I like the Norwegian approach best—baking a full-sized cake and writing the deceased's name in the frosting. Why shouldn't you have your cake and your guests eat it, too? There are so many sugary remembrance options. At Estée Lauder's funeral, waiters served chocolate-covered marshmallows on silver trays. Take some time now to think about what type of funeral confection your guests might enjoy.

Bottoms Up

Drinking is an excellent funeral activity, a centuries-old tradition in many cultures, and a great way for your guests to unwind and get to know each other.

Wine is fine, especially if you and your guests are connoisseurs, but really, I think death calls for the hard stuff. Gin, vodka, Scotch. Top-shelf in all cases. Rum is okay if you're having a beach-themed send-off. Mojitos are pretty festive. It's up to you. Name your poison, and keep it flowing. Better yet, create your own signature funeral drink. Your team can lead guests in toasts and shots, and, if you'd like, your officiate can find ways to incorporate your favorite spirits into your funeral observances.

It should be obvious that a funeral is no place for silly, nancy-girl drinks. You went through the inconvenience of dying and still took time to plan a fantastic farewell party. Your guests should understand that fruity umbrella drinks and wine coolers are not adequate beverages to honor you. If you're having a themed funeral and want to include a festive drink, do so, but set some guidelines about beverage accessories. Champagne is, of course, always appropriate.

Don't forget to have some alternative beverages—fresh-squeezed juices and sparkling water—on hand for non-drinkers. Also, don't let your caterer or team members forget to recycle the booze bottles.

Don't Forget the Details

If you think about the best parties you've attended, excluding all that occurred before age 25 and involved a keg, it's the little things that make guests feel special. Remind your team to include a few details that will mean a lot to your guests. They should want for nothing!

> ❧ *Coat check.* There's nothing more irritating than coming to an event and having to worry about

leaving your jacket or purse unattended. Hey, even friends of friends can be thieves. Also, if it's a long event, guests might want a change of clothes— something more formal for the funeral ball, and something kicky and fun for the beach bonfire.

- *Parking.* There should be adequate parking. Valet parking is always appreciated.
- *Permits.* Make sure your team submits all the necessary permits for every end-of-life event. The show must go on.
- *Tissues.* People will cry. Provide plenty of tissues and wastebaskets.
- *Restrooms.* Make sure the venue has nice, clean, accessible restrooms, as well as extra restrooms for the ladies. I shouldn't have to tell you that any outdoor event should be near a building with restrooms. Porta-Potties are tacky, smelly, and depressing.
- *Lotions and libations.* Little touches, like providing nice hand lotion and pocket-sized bottles of gin in the bathrooms will make guests feel pampered.
- *Snacks.* Have bowls of snacks in every room at all times. And plenty of water.
- *Drivers.* Always have a few designated drivers on hand so that guests can drink as much as they need to and still get home safely.
- *Help.* Hire a few college students to serve as your funeral concierges. They can run errands for guests and generally be on hand to provide instructions and support your team.

Start Planning Now

What can you do to help your guests be more comfortable at the party of your life?

- Describe special amenities and attractions your guests might like.

- Make a list of potential menu items.

- Design your funeral cookie or cake.

- Decide on a funeral drink.

- Store information in your funeral box.

CHAPTER 11

Bye-Bye Bling

Your Funeral Gift Bags

*N*ow that you've addressed your guests' basic mind and body needs, it's time to think of their spirits. What can you do to soothe their grieving hearts? Bring on the bling!

Parting Presents

There isn't a post-Oscars fête or even a child's birthday party today that doesn't include gift bags. Half the fun and intrigue of attending a fancy party is finding out what's in the gift bags. Your guests will be delighted that you thought of them. A packet of herbal teas, a handy pocket flashlight, and some fair trade organic chocolate could go a long way in reviving their heavy hearts.

I'd like to take credit for the funeral gift bag concept—and I did think of the idea before starting my funeral research—but . . . It's not really an original idea. Funeral gifts have been around as long as funerals. In medieval times, if you were lucky enough to be in the royal circle, your festive funeral attire was covered by the court. For the poor: free bread. Still, it was my idea to use bags.

In early nineteenth-century America, wealthy families gave their funeral guests scarves, handkerchiefs, gloves, or mourning rings. Family members and close friends received more sentimental souvenirs: a special locket containing a few strands of the deceased's hair or an ornate piece of jewelry made out of the deceased's hair. Lord & Taylor hasn't sold mourning gifts and apparel for quite some time, but what's stopping you from reviving and updating this thoughtful tradition with your own parting gift ideas?

The Gift of You

I want to give my guests funeral gifts they'll cherish, as well as include a few items that will make them laugh when they feel like crying. So, I'll definitely have a funeral T-shirt. There will be a photo of me on the front of the shirt, and the inscription "I went to Erika's funeral, and all I got was this lousy T-shirt" on the back. You can apply the same concept to mugs, key chains, and other less expensive gifts. Other ideas: Post-its, mouse pads, or baseball caps bearing your favorite saying and an illustration of you.

I also want to give my loved ones a little bit of me. What could be more personal? My closest friends will receive something extra in their gift bags—a small packet of my ashes, with individualized instructions for disposal. I've asked my friend Sarah to dump her portion of my ashes in the Mississippi River off of the Hennepin Avenue Bridge in Minneapolis. My Body Boss, Steph, will mail a tiny bag of me to my friends in London, who will sprinkle me into the Thames, and my friends Brian and Megan have been assigned the task of scattering their portion of my ashes in Marlborough Sound in New Zealand. Of course, I'll provide plane tickets and per diem expenses for those who have to traverse the globe to fulfill my funeral wishes.

Death Bling

If you'd like to stay close to some of your favorite people, you have options. Include personal mini-urns or ash containers in your gift bags for home or office display. How about leaving first-tier friends necklaces and pendants with tiny, hidden ash compartments?

If money is no object, have your ashes made into a diamond that can be set into a ring, earrings, or a necklace pendant. Actually, there's plenty of you to make several diamonds of all sizes, cuts, and colors. Get some serious life insurance now and your lovely wife can get the princess cut earrings you could never afford in life. You didn't last forever—but a diamond made out of you will.

Naturally, you'll want to include a CD of your funeral soundtrack in your gift bags. Then your guests can relive the party of your life whenever they miss you. Memorial videos are also very popular these days. You can play yours at one of your funeral events, post excerpts of it on your website (*after* the funeral), and stick a copy of it on DVD in each gift bag. Make your own with a home video camera, or hire someone to make the DVD of your life. There are end-trepreneurs and professional videographers available for all budgets.

Maybe you'd like to keep the rituals and audience involvement going long after the party. Include in your gift bags some items that will help your loved ones perform their own private memorial observances once they get home: a packet of wildflower seeds and a laminated, credit card-sized memory card, with your favorite quotes and the GPS coordinates of your natural burial site on one side, and a photo of you on the other. Any or all of these items will make excellent parting gifts.

Members Only

When I originally developed the funeral gift bag concept, I thought it would be nice to hand out the bags as guests entered the service, but my publisher cautioned me against this approach. In his experience with children's parties, gift bags are a way to thank guests for their gifts and entice screaming six-year-olds into leaving when the party is feeling long past over. I don't think guests need much enticing to skip out early on a funeral—unless it's a self-planned, fantastic funeral—but he does have a point. If your guests get the goods first, they may not stay as long as you'd like. Also, you don't want people fussing with their bags during the service, distracting or ignoring the performers on stage.

People always remember the gift bags. In fact, in addition to a bouncer, you'll need a seriously hard-core friend or hired hand to guard and oversee the distribution of the gift bags. People will always try to get more than one "For my spouse who couldn't attend." Up to you, but I say, you don't come to the party of my life, you don't get a gift bag.

The Bag

These days it's important to conserve resources, so take care in selecting an appropriate gift bag that can be reused and repurposed after your funeral.

Long after the chocolates have been consumed, your guests will remember you every time they perform the good deed of bringing their own bag to the grocery store.

Photo Ops

While you're reviving Victorian funeral customs, why not revisit another funeral tradition: mourning photos.

Back then you couldn't perish without a few good death photos. There was the requisite photo of the deceased, laid out in the casket. There were group photos of family members surrounding the deceased (who, by the way, was dressed to kill) in a well-appointed parlor or photo studio. Then there were elaborately staged photos where the deceased might be propped up in a chair or even into a standing position, photographed alone or with family, just like old times. My favorites are the families gathered on the front porch, with an empty chair representing the deceased and one or more of the family members pointing toward the sky. Inscriptions were also incorporated into some photos. Today, thanks to digital photography and Photoshop, you have hundreds of options for your posthumous photos.

THE PARTY *of* MOLLY WHITE'S LIFE

MOLLY WHITE
1928–
Ohio, USA

PLANS: I have not made any plans yet but I did plan my husband's memorial, since he did not leave behind instructions. We all sat in a circle in the living room and everyone took turns talking. I kind of like the idea of just the family involved. The simpler, the better. Gather here and spread my ashes in the woods behind my house.

I think my sons can figure out music that they know I would like. And there should be a nice meal—casseroles and plenty of wine and beer. The atmosphere should not be formal at all. I know the Montessori school will probably have some kind of service for me since I have been involved with them for about fifty years.

LEGAL: I have it in writing not to prolong my life on machines. It's good to think about these things in advance.

Your ancestors really knew how to ratchet up the drama and get more emotional mileage out of their deceased relatives. Let your survivors do the same! What could be more festive than having a photographer on hand to document your last party?

Your team could recreate a Victorian sitting room with black mourning costumes and props, or come up with another themed setting. Individuals, couples, and small groups could have their portraits taken—just as they did at prom when you were kids—all in the name of *you*. You can even be in the photo if you'd like (and if you think your guests can handle it). There's you and your yoga teacher at your deathbed; there you are, lying in state on your Herman Miller sofa in the living room of your posh modular home; there are your two BFFs painting your cardboard casket at your home wake party; there's Cousin Billy kissing the side of your urn (of course, if you're cremated, you can easily join the party and share the spotlight with your guests); there are your spouse and kids holding hands at your natural burial site. The photographic possibilities are endless. (Some people might find these ideas a tad macabre; others will appreciate the Gothic humor of it. Only you can decide what's "real fun" for you and your guests.)

As they were so long ago, your mourning photos will become cherished mementos for your guests, as well as for your loved ones who were unable to attend the party of your life due to illness (there is no other excuse for missing someone's life celebration). Include a scrapbook in your gift bag so your guests can keep their favorite funeral photos, as well as newspaper clippings about your funeral, your obituary, the funeral program, and other items from your final party safe for generations to come. If you can't afford to include the books, sell them on your funeral website. Your friends will buy them. (You can mark up the price a bit and let your friends know that a percentage of sales will benefit your favorite local charity.)

Another way to live on in your guests' hearts and lives: have your team create a mourning calendar with your photos. Then your guests can keep track of your remembrance activities throughout the coming year. Your mourning photos can also be used for posters, buttons, and screen savers. Naturally, you'll want to make all of this content available for download at your funeral website for guests who would rather view it on their iPads than assemble a paper scrapbook.

Post-You Mailings

Whether your end-of-life celebrations last for two hours or two weeks, your guests will grieve for months, if not years. Anniversaries, class reunions, and other notable dates will be especially difficult for them. So why not stay in touch from beyond?

One fun project you can work on now is preparing a grief kit your team can use to help you keep in touch with your loved ones after you're gone. Your kit might include a letter to your inner circle for your death anniversary, a series of postcards that can be sent to your guest list on a recurring basis, and a "director's cut" of your funeral video. Your post-you postcard is a wonderful way to share loving affirmations and practical tips, as well as highlight your funeral logo and tagline, which will help you keep the party of your life in their minds. I've already designed my mailing: a black note card with the following handwritten message, in white letters, "I miss you, too."

If you don't have a funeral team to carry out these mailings, there are companies that will send letters or emails to your loved ones. Another popular idea is writing love letters now. Tell your loved ones how you feel about them, and store these letters in your funeral box. You can personalize messages for each of your closest friends and family members, and use a general letter for fourth-tier friends, acquaintances, colleagues, and former classmates.

If you're not sure what to say or how to begin, hire a professional. However, if you're relatively young, a parent, and tragically perishing from a terminal illness, you'll probably have no problem coming up with love letter material for your children to open on upcoming birthdays when you won't be there to celebrate with them. If you are dying, start keeping a journal or at least making voice recordings with your iPod or other digital voice recorder. It may seem morbid, but your loved ones will cherish any words you leave behind.

If you end up in hospice care, ask them if they send post-you mailings. You may want to opt out if you're going to send your own card. I think an occasional personal message from you could be charming and much more meaningful. But you know your audience best.

I'd advise you not to stay in touch too frequently, or your whimsical beyond-the-grave reminders could start getting creepy. Self-obsession is one thing, but timing is key if you want them to share your sense of humor. Maybe you could try having cards sent at irregular intervals. Mix it up a bit. Give your loved ones the time and space to miss you.

Start Planning Now

When you were alive they gave you so much; it's time for you to give back. What would help your loved ones cope with their loss of you?

- Make a list of items for your gift bags.

- Write a draft of your goodbye letter and remembrance postcards.

- Get started on your video tribute.

- Describe what your team should include in your grief kit.

- Store information in your funeral box.

CHAPTER 12

Sideshows and Show-Stoppers

Good Drama vs. Bad Drama

ven the best-laid plans can be disrupted, and that's okay. Sometimes it's the unscripted dramas that can enliven an end-of-life celebration.

Funeral Funny Business

There's just no telling how your loved ones will react to your death or how they'll behave during the various remembrance events, especially if alcohol is involved. Fatigue, grief, and over-stimulation can take a toll. Social conventions will also be at play. Some of your guests will cry, others will remain stone-faced and stoic. It's quite likely that at least one of your guests will act out in some way, creating an uncomfortable but potentially riveting emotional scene.

My friend Mary witnessed such an event at her great-uncle's funeral, a service drenched in Southern tradition. The minute the ceremony began, her great-aunt performed her mourning role to the hilt, keening like a true Southern widow. She also made a run for the casket, shook it a few times, then attempted to jump in to join her "beloved." Never mind that she had hated her spouse while he was alive. Naturally, her relatives saw this coming (as she knew they would and as they knew she'd know they would) and stopped her before she even lifted a leg.

That's the kind of funeral drama guests are lucky to see. It's better than anything on the Lifetime Movie Network. Even if an outburst by the deceased's next-of-kin may initially make some guests feel awkward, it just might be a necessary, perhaps even unconsciously performed, function that breaks the tension in the air. It's a cue to guests that the most bereaved party is getting what he or she needs out of the event.

Guests Behaving Badly

Of course, there's a difference between good drama and bad drama. Good drama adds spontaneity, perks up weary guests, and encourages people to get in touch with their deepest feelings. Good drama can shift the energy and redirect the focus during tense or limp moments. It also makes for a great story after the fact. Bad drama is never a good idea or a good time.

It's funny if your uncle Tom gets a little drunk and his toupee comes loose. It's not funny if he gets drunk, wets his pants, and makes a move on your best friend. It's also not funny if your dead aunt's alcoholic ex-boyfriend has the limo driver stop for a six-pack en route to your grandfather's burial. It's especially not funny if your 84-year-old uncle and 92-year-old aunt (not married to each other, just connected through their siblings' marriage) get in a shoving match at your grandmother's graveside ceremony over something that happened in 1929. (I made up the first two scenarios—the other two actually happened. Truth is, indeed, stranger than fiction. And why is it that aunts and uncles seem to provide so many funeral dramas?)

Nobody wants to witness truly inappropriate behavior. It's

okay to test the edge—who hasn't after a few drinks?—but you want your guests to enjoy themselves. And behave. After all, it's your day, and nobody should distract your guests from focusing on you.

Unexpected Deaths

In order to get the funeral you want and deserve, you might also want to have an emergency plan in place. That way if someone becomes ill, sustains a serious injury, or dies at your funeral or at any of your send-off parties, your team, bouncer, or medics can remove him or her from the venue as quickly and discreetly as possible. You want to keep the focus on you but also protect your guests from additional stress and trauma.

If the stricken guest is well-known and his illness or injury is mild, your officiate or family liaison may update the party with news that's he's stable, well, and resting peacefully at the

---

THE PARTY *of* CYRUS FARMER'S LIFE

CYRUS FARMER
1968–
California, USA

PLANS: The only thing I'm sure of is that my wife and I have made a pact. If we're still married at the time of our deaths, we will be cremated. If I go first, she'll hang onto my ashes (and vice versa if she goes first—if we go together, no issues). On our wedding anniversary the following year, our kids will scatter our ashes together at a designated location.

local hospital. That will help everyone relax and enjoy the party of your life.

Also, be prepared for freak accidents. In Los Angeles, a policeman participating in a funeral cortège for a colleague was killed when a tree was struck by lightning and fell on his car. Of course, these tragedies are very sad, but your party must go on. The unfortunate guest or official will have his own party on his own day. Don't forget, funerals for policemen and other civic protectors are very formal affairs. Your fallen soldier will have his day, too.

On the other hand, you don't know whose life might be saved by attending your funeral. A couple from the South escaped death by attending a funeral out of state the exact day a tornado ripped through their trailer park, demolishing everything on the property and killing all inhabitants present. Life is a game of chance, and as REO Speedwagon so aptly sang, "You have to roll with the changes."

Start Planning Now

- ❧ Anticipate any potential bad drama, and make sure you have people in place to deal with unruly guests.

- ❧ Flag any guests on your list who might cause problems.

- ❧ Leave a note for your team to consider hiring a bouncer if necessary.

- ❧ Assign a team member to bring a first aid kit, flashlights, flares, and cell phone chargers (AC and DC), as well as the phone numbers for AAA or other emergency assistance services.

- ❧ Store information in your funeral box.

"According to most studies, people's number-one fear is public speaking. Number two is death. Death is number two. Does that sound right? This means to the average person, if you go to a funeral, you're better off in the casket than doing the eulogy."

—JERRY SEINFELD (1954–),
stand-up comedian, actor, and author

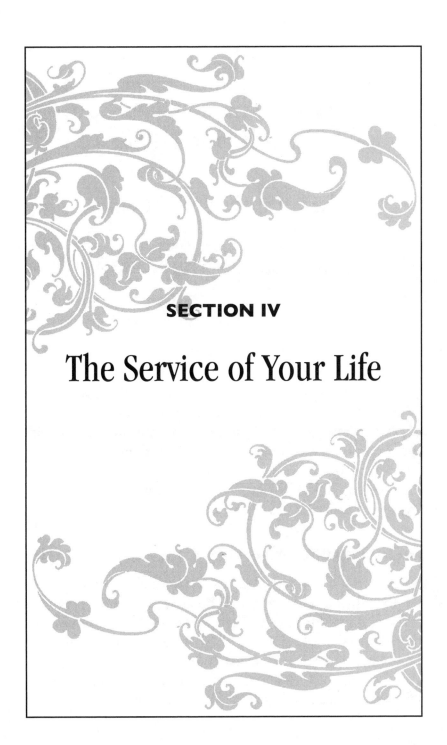

SECTION IV

The Service of Your Life

CHAPTER 13

Services For All Sorts

God or Mod

With so many celebration alternatives, you might start thinking that you don't need or want a funeral "service." The thing is, the service isn't just for you—it's for the people you leave behind. The other thing is, if you don't leave plans for a service (and even if you explicitly request that there be no service), someone might have one for you anyway. Best if you take control while you can.

Give the People What They Want

Faced with the huge void that your absence leaves in their lives, your friends and family will be in serious pain, and they'll want an outlet for their feelings. Before they can take a whack at the funeral piñata at your memorial carnival or jump into the bunny hop line at your funeral fandango, they'll need to experience a sense of occasion around your passing. Something sort of sacred. Personalize your funeral all you want—keep it brief if that's what you'd like—but you might want to consider including some type of ceremony in your party lineup to help everyone start processing the tragedy of losing you.

People will attend your funeral for many reasons: they loved you; they liked you; they want to see if you're really dead; they sat in the cubicle next to you at work and felt obligated to come (or not, if you have an invitation-only funeral); they were raised to show respect for the deceased's survivors and want to honor you and your family even if they hardly knew you; they lived next door to you; they're dating your neighbor and she wanted an escort; now that your wife is free they want to be first in line to help her pick up the pieces and start a new life . . . whatever.

Bottom line: your survivors will have some expectations around your death. It won't kill you to honor that. Self-planning is good. Selfish planning is bad.

A Better Bye-Bye

If you don't leave behind some details for a service or, worse, don't adequately choreograph your exit, you leave the door wide open for someone to plan a funeral ceremony for you that says nothing about your life. Then you risk alienating or boring your survivors, robbing them of their emotional needs around your demise. You might also leave family members at odds about how to honor you. Then you miss out on some serious, focused attention.

I know a woman whose family dutifully honored their mother's wishes with a direct burial and no funeral. Three years after her mother's death, she's still grieving and frustrated over the additional loss of missing out on a service where her family could have come together to share their fond memories and support each other in their sorrow. Her siblings don't share her feelings, so she has finally decided to have her own personal memorial event in a quiet wooded setting as soon as things slow down a bit at work. You might think you're being noble by skipping any type of ceremony or ritual, but if you have people in your life who love you, let them do something for you (and for themselves). Just make sure you control it as much as possible by recruiting a crack funeral team or advocate to manage the event.

You'll also want to consult with a funeral director, celebrant, clergy member, party planner, yoga teacher, Wiccan priestess, or other spiritual and entertainment guides who can advise you (or your team, when the time comes) on some basic ceremony formats. Your idea of "simple" might not be well-executed by your survivors. My good friend and funeral team member Frank attended a colleague's bare-bones, self-planned funeral a few years ago, and it was a total bomb. As the deceased had requested, everything was extremely low budget and "no fuss." The brief service was held at a small funeral home chapel and consisted of a few friends mumbling awkwardly through their eulogies, then playing a couple of classic rock songs on a boom box. It was a sad, unorganized, unsatisfying affair that lasted about 10 minutes. You could say that the funeral was a success because the deceased got what he asked for, but the truth is—your guests deserve to have their funeral needs met, too (or at least acknowledged). Frank felt uncomfortable and embarrassed for everyone involved. Remember, a bad funeral is like bad theater—not worth the price of admission. You can keep it simple and inexpensive and still give the audience a good show.

Secular or Spiritual Can Be Spectacular

Traditionally, the American funeral has been a religious service, which by nature just isn't very festive or unique. Yours doesn't have to be that way. You and your loved ones deserve a farewell with more pop.

Maybe you'd like a religious service. Maybe you'd prefer a secular service. Or maybe you'd just like to exclude a few religious customs that don't have meaning for you. You can go with God, have a modern, secular ceremony filled with your own unique rituals and customs, or find a balance between the two. Just because you don't have a religious background doesn't mean you can't have a spiritual service or that you can't borrow from religious traditions with colorful outfits and sparkly tableware. Likewise, just because you were raised Catholic or Lutheran or Jewish or Muslim doesn't mean you can't have a pagan ceremony.

Certainly, it should be obvious to you at this point that a secular service at a secular venue gives you the most freedom in

---

THE PARTY *of* AMELIA MORRIS ENRIQUEZ'S LIFE

AMELIA MORRIS ENRIQUEZ
1959–
Georgia, USA

PARTY: I want my memorial party held in Atlanta, and all of my friends better be there. Also, it better be a dance party!

VIEWS: I request an autopsy. I'm an organ donor; I want everyone to honor that.

LEGAL: I've completed a living will, and I don't want to be kept alive as a vegetable.

DISPOSAL: I want to be cremated, and I want a pinch of my ashes sprinkled off of Devil's Courthouse, a rocky outcrop off of the Blue Ridge Parkway in North Carolina. I want the rest of my ashes put in a box selected by my two best girlfriends and my sister.

selecting an officiate, the readings, music, funeral party games, artistic installations, dramatic reenactments, and rituals involving fire and water. On the other hand, you might belong to a fun-filled faith that's all about celebrating life at death. The important thing is to get what you want and not be limited or coerced by outside forces, family pressure, or anyone else's idea of what's appropriate.

Pleasing Your Parents

If your sayonara style is a jarring departure from your family's faith, you can modify your plans to suit your loved ones. Unless you have a stone cold heart or your parents were really evil, advise your funeral team in advance that it's okay to accommodate your folks on a few points if you expire before they do. Outliving your children is the worst kind of bummer, so they deserve a break.

For example, your Celebration Master can let your parents know that Pastor Brown is certainly welcome to say a few words at your Led Zeppelin-themed funeral, and, yes, Aunt Millie can play her favorite banjo tunes, as she has at every family funeral since 1965, but the cover band starts exactly at 9:00 PM.

If your loved ones will only be satisfied with a religious service and you want to please them, maybe you're okay with leaving a few details up to them because, after the service, your team can still host the party of your life. Then again, you're the one who has to die, so maybe you shouldn't worry so much about what other people are going to think.

Building Connections

The key to pulling off a personalized funeral that your guests will remember until they die is helping them understand the various elements of your carefully orchestrated service (the party will be the easy part).

If your loved ones are actually part of your life now (as

opposed to the guests who might not have seen you since fourth grade), they probably won't be surprised by any of your funky funeral festivities. However, some people, especially churchgoers, may still have traditional expectations around the event. That's okay. You can be creative and still connect with all of your guests.

Keep in mind that everyone there will want to feel that they're doing their part. They also need to leave the service in a better state than when they arrived. Nobody likes feeling left out or confused in a sacred ceremony, so if you're mixing it up, make sure you have a rock solid officiate who can guide the program. Help your guests follow along by explaining some of your more unusual rituals on the back of the program or in the invitation booklet. If you're replacing standard hymns with the songs from *Quadrophenia*, make sure each guest has the liner notes so they can sing along. (After the service, your ashes can be carried to the sea on a tricked-out Vespa.)

Also, many religions utilize similar rites and customs, such as burning candles and singing or chanting. Even if you've altered these rituals or imbued them with new meaning, your guests will probably be fine. (If they don't like your ritual, they can practice it with their own religion or spiritual preferences in mind. Many guests may be too old to catch your symbolism anyway. The special touches are for you and for those who knew you best.)

The important thing is to create a service that has your character all over it. Create a new type of communion with yerba maté and vegan scones, have your officiate wear a feathery headdress or hand-carved mask, ask your brother to read "Howl," include a screening of a Spalding Gray monologue. It's you're funeral; pack it full of your favorite things. Let your team and officiate worry about the details.

If you're still absolutely dead set against a funeral service, that's okay. You can include a brief memorial ritual or a few eulogies at your graveside or ash-scattering picnic, or at one of your other end-of-life events.

Death Bennies

If you were a public employee, soldier, or politician, you might be entitled to benefits like a seriously statesman-like graveside ceremony and discounts on plots (or even free burial) in a designated cemetery, where you'll be laid to rest with your peers. Such an occasion would certainly give your survivors an immediate and formal event with which to honor you. Who knows, maybe planning assistance comes with the burial bennies. (There also might be a long waiting list for the choice cemeteries, so look into this now.)

Even if you weren't involved in organized civic or national service, you still might have lived a life exciting or worthy enough to inspire government officials to throw you a state funeral. It happened to world-famous mountaineer Sir Edmund Hillary. (Although he was a WWII veteran, I'm sure it was his fame as an explorer and his philanthropic efforts that inspired Britain to appoint him Knight Commander of the Order of the British Empire, and New Zealand, his home country, to put his face on their five-dollar bill, and, when the time came, throw him a funeral fit for a king.)

If you're a veteran, contact the Department of Veterans Affairs (www.cem.va.gov) to find out about your death benefits. Also important: let your survivors know now whether or not you want to use these benefits or if you have another memorial or burial scenario in mind. Just because it's there doesn't mean you have to take it. President Ford eschewed several elements of his rightful state funeral perks for a more low-key exit. You might have loved your time in the service, but don't want to be buried in a military cemetery because you have your heart set on a certain flashy, non-regulation headstone. Decide now. Write it down.

Your spouse might receive some perks, too. If Social Security still exists by the time you pass away, your spouse may be entitled to a one-time death benefit. The current payment is $255. It's not much, but it's enough for a hot stone massage and a facial—something anyone could enjoy after working hard to make your funeral happen.

Just Don't

Just in case there are a few "I don't want" items that haven't occurred to you, please allow me to advise you against a few funeral ideas.

There is one type of funeral you should never consider: a clown funeral. Unless you are a clown and all of your guests will be clowns, just don't do it. Even then, it's a bad idea. I know a young man whose stepfather was a clown. He attended his stepfather's clown funeral and confirmed what I expected: the event was kind of creepy and full of bitter, broken-down, boozing clowns. He left before it was over. That is not fun for anyone. All the world does *not* love a clown.

I also advise against a double funeral. You may want to instruct your team that even if you die at the exact same time and place as your favorite person, you will need your own, separate memorial celebration. If they must plan back-to-back events to make it easier on out-of-town guests, so be it, but the focus of your special day should be on you. While you're at it, inform your funeral team that pairing up your funeral with a wedding, birthday party, or any other type of event will only distract your guests and dilute the concepts you've worked so hard to develop.

I should also add here that your funeral should not be too esoteric or enigmatic. Your loved ones put up with your weird behavior when you were alive; they shouldn't have to work too hard at your funeral just to understand what's going on. A little intrigue is one thing, but there has to be a payoff for them at some point. A funeral that's all about the mystery of you isn't fun—it's a drag.

Bottom line: don't clown around about your end-of-life plans. Take your death and your survivors' grief seriously, and exit with style.

Start Planning Now

Decide now: God or mod? Pagan or posh? How will you say goodbye?

- Describe your dream funeral service.

- If you don't want a service, describe an alternate observance your survivors can practice at one of your end-of-life events (or on their own).

- Leave instructions for any aspects of your funeral that might need explaining.

- Clarify your religious or spiritual preferences (or bans).

- Make a list of things you do *not* want in your funeral service or ceremony.

- Let your survivors know if you're entitled to military (or other) honors and whether or not you want these benefits.

- Store information in your funeral box.

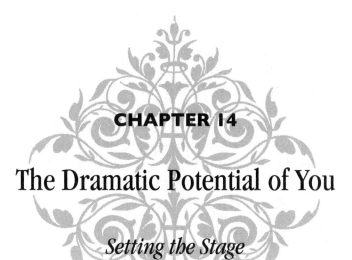

CHAPTER 14

The Dramatic Potential of You

Setting the Stage

aybe you've never considered the dramatic poten-tial of a you-centered event. Or maybe, like me, you've been waiting your whole life to plan your per-fect funeral. It's the only day of your life when you'll receive every-one's undivided attention. So take advantage of it.

All About You

No matter how good or bad you were in life, you'll never be better or more interesting than in death. If you were smart, kind, and charming, your survivors, in their grief, will remem-ber you as smarter, kinder, and more charming than you really were. Even if you were a cantankerous old fart, your most irritat-ing behavior and unpleasant habits will be remembered fondly as endearing, eccentric traits that made you special (or at the very least, they'll make excuses for you—"Poor guy, no wonder he was cranky, living all those years with shrapnel embedded in his ass").

Either way, you win.

You will also never receive as much airtime in life as you will in death. Consider the example of Princess Diana. A mere 750 million watched her wedding; two and a half billion people tuned in for her funeral. You may not have the global reach of a royal (or the budget to produce such regal fanfare), but don't underestimate the impact you've had on the people in your life. Your loyal subjects will definitely tune in for whatever type of farewell you choose for yourself.

Your friends and family will really feel the pain. People who liked you but never really got to know you will see how deeply your inner circle is grieving and wish they'd taken the time to know you better. Third- and fourth-tier friends will wish they'd done a better job of staying in touch. Even people who didn't like you and strangers who happen to skim your obituary in the paper on the train ride to work will have warm feelings for you. Grudges, petty arguments, and jealousies will all fade away as everyone you know comes together to mourn their loss of you.

Mourning Becomes Them

Your demise will also inspire and motivate people. Your survivors will start thinking about their lives, their own mortality, and what they'd like to do with the time they have left. Some will admire how bold, adventurous, and independent you were, and realize that they need to make changes in their lives.

Your Aunt Sheila will finally take that trip to the Galapagos Islands. Your best friend will finally leave her lying, cheating husband and start a new life in Santa Fe. Your cousin will recall your dedication to the environment and become an organic farmer.

Even some of your not-so-positive traits might encourage your survivors to consider their life choices. Your not-so-secret Vicodin addiction will serve as a cautionary tale for your pothead nephew—just the warning sign he needs to straighten up and fly right.

For better or worse, the party of your life will unify, inform, and, hopefully, entertain the folks you leave behind. So, you need to take advantage of the post-mortem energy surrounding your demise, and of your own dramatic potential, to produce an event (or events) that will leave your guests with lasting memories of you, as well as a renewed passion for life.

Your Goodbye Gala

Nobody would ever say so, but everyone loves a good funeral. We all have a morbid curiosity about these matters. We all have a primal need to gather, participate in symbolic rituals, and connect with each other over our shared grief.

As your guests arrive, there will be a buzz of anticipation in the air, not to mention an awful lot of pent-up tension and anguish just waiting to bust out. Your guests will also wonder who else will be there and if their wardrobe choices are sufficiently mourning-ish without being drab or gloomy.

Despite their sorrow, they won't be above wondering who will come with whom. It's still a social event, and they'll still be titillated by finding out who has coupled or uncoupled since the

---

THE PARTY *of* KATIE YATES'S LIFE

KATIE YATES
1965–
Connecticut, USA

PLANS: Burn my body at the seaside, or in the mountains. Serve wine. Tell my kids to rock on and relax. Sing a little.

last funeral or retirement party. Most of all, they'll want to be moved. They'll want a good cathartic cry. They'll need plenty of opportunities for cathartic laughter. So give it to them.

It's up to you to design (or hire someone who can design) a memorial tribute that will harness, sustain, and direct the swirl of emotions into a coherent, dynamic production that will keep your loved ones tuned in, pumped up, and on their toes.

A well-planned ceremony that highlights your best self will show your survivors that you have accepted your death, and now, so can they. It can also set the tone for the other funeral events in your send-off series.

Knowing Me, Knowing You

Naturally, your life celebration should be unabashedly all about you, but to pull off a truly meaningful farewell you need to understand and anticipate what your guests will be feeling and thinking. Just because you're able to put the "F-U-N" back in funeral doesn't mean that your survivors won't initially be devastated by losing you.

The key to a successful farewell service is maintaining the dramatic tension throughout the event. You want to keep your guests interested or at least engaged until the balloons are released, or your favorite song blares out of the loudspeakers, or the parade marshal appears to march your guests down main street—whatever signals the end of the ceremony and the beginning of the next celebration phase.

Your service shouldn't gloss over the cloud of grief in the air, but help your guests tap into their hearts and feel the joy of loving you. You don't want them to think too much, but simply sit back and feel the love while enjoying the spectacle around them.

Ultimately, a successful funeral does much more than merely grab your guests' attention. Your carefully chosen rituals, eulogies, and other observances should all help create a comforting, stimulating, and interactive atmosphere in which your guests will feel bonded to each other. You want each guest to feel part of a giant love embrace in which everyone loves you, each other, and their own special selves.

Having said that, you can't merely rely on your guests' raw emotions, or even on your obsessively planned funeral soundtrack (impressive and eclectic as it may be) to carry the event. You need a tight script and a skilled officiate to help set the tone and keep your celebration on pace. (See more about selecting an officiate in the next chapter).

There's No Business Like Show Business

The best funerals incorporate elements of film, theater, and dance, as well as other forms of creative expression. Depending on your funeral goals, your potential attendees, and your venue, you can also seek theatrical inspiration from a variety of public events—graduation ceremonies, political conventions, and bullfights, to name a few—to soothe, stir, engross, cajole, provoke, beguile, charm, and incite your guests.

If you can choreograph a dramatic arc worthy of an Oscar-winning film, your guests are going to be glued to their seats. Throw in the charisma and upbeat songs of a Broadway musical, and they'll start tapping their feet along to the beat. Sometimes actions speak louder than words. Never underestimate the emotional impact of a jazzy tap riff, daring aerial acrobatics, or a martial arts demonstration to thrill and motivate your guests.

It's not about planning a flashy, extravagant affair, unless, of course, you have the budget. It's about using all of the resources available to you to create a whirl of energy that will define your special day. A simple ceremony can work just fine. Pomp and glamour are less important than creating your own individual funeral chi from which every invitation, streamer, and crab cake will flow.

Of course, stylistic and technical aspects such as lighting and set design can go a long way to enhance your efforts. Every member of your funeral team, as well as the players in the actual event, will be responsible for assembling the various elements into a stylish, magnificent show.

A word of warning—nobody will be impressed with your B.A. in theatre from Snooty University, so you can forget about a *Waiting for Godot* or *Marat/Sade* service. It's never a good idea to give people reasons to walk out of a funeral.

Turn Pain into Passion

Since your guests will all want to demonstrate their feelings for you with a gesture of remembrance, why not think up a few ways to involve your guests in your favorite causes and campaigns?

Use your final farewell to save the whales or feed the children. Ask your guests to gift an impoverished village with a team of goats, or one of Dean Kamen's water purifiers, or the funds to build a school or clinic. Nobody's going to deny a dead person his or her last wishes.

Maybe you'd just like to create a little more awareness about some very important social issues. Use your funeral program to remind your guests about the many ways they can reduce their carbon footprints. Better yet, have your program printed on compostable, seed-embedded card stock that guests can plant when they get home. Within a few weeks, your loved ones will be reminded of you and your eco values as they watch your farewell flowers bloom. At the very least, your seeds of rebirth will be packed with life-affirming symbolism.

Finally, if you die from a tragic accident that could have been prevented by better road signage or traffic laws, or from a rare disease, or from an illness caused by workplace exposure to carcinogens, your new status will motivate your guests to contact their congressmen about creating tougher drunk driving laws or allocating more funding for medical research. (Your team can place petitions and donation cards next to the guest book.)

With a little forethought, you can help turn your survivors' grief into action, giving them a productive and generous outlet for their pain. It's too late for you, but they can still help others.

Start Planning Now

What's your dramatic potential? And how far does it reach?

- Describe live performances, movies, or other art forms that capture the dramatic edge you'd like expressed in your farewell party.

- List the emotions you'd like to evoke at your various end-of-life events.

- Describe the charitable or political actions you'd like your guests to take on your behalf.

- Store information in your funeral box.

CHAPTER 15

Who Runs the Show?

Selecting an Officiate

Whether your service is secular or spiritual, you'll probably want (and your team will appreciate having) a professional overseeing the show. A trained officiate should be able to gracefully guide your guests through various observances, as well as direct an engaging program shimmering with your distinctive funeral energy.

At Your Service

There's a reason most funerals have traditionally been officiated by members of the clergy—they know what they're doing and they know what to say. Even if they don't know anything about the deceased, they have stock readings, hymns, and scripture to use and they know how to organize and pace a funeral service.

If you belong to a church or want a church service, that's one way to go. Talk to your minister, rabbi, priest, lama, vicar, guru, or chaplain soon about how she or he can help you create a one-of-a-kind life tribute. Better to find out now if your chosen officiate and venue can accommodate aerial installations and speakers that go to 11. A good funeral will have its own rhythm and soul. A good officiate will help balance the emotional peaks with calming observances and rituals.

If religion isn't your bag, or if you don't know anyone in the clergy, don't settle for a rent-a-pastor. Find a celebrant who can help your team put the "F-U-N" back in funeral.

Celebrant Good Times

Certified celebrants are trained in planning and officiating a variety of milestone events, including funerals. A celebrant can carry the show or assist you (or your team, once you're gone) in creating any type of ceremony you'd like. As more people plan personalized exits, celebrants are becoming a popular choice.

Because celebrants aren't tied to a single philosophy or a specific religion, they may offer you a wider range of memorial possibilities. Your celebrant can help you plan a secular or religious service, a Tai Chi service, a Bon Jovi service—or no service at all, but a full-tilt memorial Macarena party. Maybe you'd like a few spiritual elements in your service, but want to skip a sermon. Maybe you'd like to include observances from cultures or faiths you know little about. Your best bet for a secular service, or an unconventional memorial ceremony, is probably a celebrant.

Depending on an individual celebrant's training, she or he might have more to offer than event planning and officiating skills. Some celebrants are also members of the clergy; others are trained death midwives who can provide you and your family with support during your final days. The celebrant I plan to hire for my funeral is also a licensed funeral director and a home funeral guide, so she'll be able to file the necessary end-of-life paperwork with the county, help my survivors host a home-based funeral, arrange for my disposal, and manage the rest of my death details. (To learn more about celebrant training and certification, check out www.celebrantinstitute.org and www.insightbooks.com.)

Take the time before you're too old or too ill to interview a few people who can advise you on the most effective way to stage your life celebration and, when the time comes, direct the festivities.

The Show Must Go On

It may seem fitting to ask friends to officiate at your service, especially if they've been certified by an online "ministry" to perform weddings and funerals, but don't do it unless the people (or person) you recruit actually have the chops to deliver a sustained performance, from the entrance music to the closing remarks. Most people will need a professional involved.

I'm lucky to have several qualified friends on my funeral team who will co-officiate if I die young, which I don't plan on doing. My friend and Event Planner Brian (first-tier) is an actor, director, writer, and the funniest person I know. He can easily produce and emcee the event. My friend Carolyn (also first-tier) is a

---

THE PARTY *of* STEVE CLARK'S LIFE

STEVE CLARK
1947–
Washington, USA

EVENT: A combined outdoor funeral and memorial party on Mount Erie, open to all. It'll be a potluck party with wine and beer. I'd like my friend Mark Backlund to officiate the ceremony.

THEME: Connection to the Larger.

READINGS: "The Rose" by Roethke, "Ithaka" by Cavafy,

Wiccan priestess; she'll craft a personalized ceremony full of exciting and effective rituals. Together, under the guidance of my celebrant, they'll make sure I get the funeral I want and deserve.

If my officiates should happen to die before me, or are too overcome with grief to perform, I have a backup plan. My friend Rene is an American Baptist minister. She's a professional and, like an emergency room doctor, will be able to put her emotions aside (although she said she might cry at my service, and that's okay with me) in order to step in and take care of my guests. Because we're friends, Rene would even be willing to officiate at my funeral without mentioning God, the bible, or anything remotely religious. I want all the talk to be about me.

According to Rene, most members of clergy probably wouldn't be willing to perform such a service for someone just walking in off of the street, but if you have a friend or family member in the biz, ask her now if she'd be comfortable performing a secular service for you.

---

	and selections from Rilke, Mary Oliver, and Whitman.
SOUNDTRACK:	The Byrds.
RELIGION:	The power of nature is my religion, à la John Muir.
DISPOSAL:	Cremation. I want some of my ashes scattered on Mount Erie, some on top of Mount Rainier, and some on my mother's grave in Owensville, Indiana.
LEGAL:	I have a medical directive and a medical power of attorney in place.

All You Do Is Talk Talk

If you don't have an officiate who knows you well (and even if you do), make sure you instruct your team to give that person plenty of personal anecdotes to share. Ministers and emcees love having that type of input because it gives them the information they need to connect with the crowd in a meaningful way.

Most of the funerals I've attended were boring because the clergy in charge clearly didn't know the deceased and the cookie-cutter format said nothing to me about the person I'd loved and lost. That's why I got involved in my grandmother's funeral. The service was simple and brief, conducted by a friend of my mother's, a laid-back Congregational minister. There wasn't a sermon; instead, he told the stories my parents and I had shared with him. Hearing him talk about my grandmother in a real way was truly a comfort, especially since one of the stories highlighted—very subtly, of course—that I had clearly been her favorite grandchild.

Sometimes stories can take on a life of their own. My friend Rene is a big fan of open mic funerals; eulogy-heavy services are very popular at her parish. She recommends including in your ceremony as much about yourself as possible. Your officiate can schedule as much or as little eulogy time as you'd like, depending on your guest list, your funeral goals, and how many memorial events you're planning. You might want to save some of the eulogies for the party of your life or for your funeral banquet.

I love the idea of an all-eulogy service. If you have a lot of friends and colleagues and don't really want to plan much of a funeral, this approach can be enjoyable and fulfilling for your guests. Another bonus of a eulogy-based service: your guests will feel closer to each other. By the end of the event, your childhood friends and your college friends will share a bond. They'll seek each other out at the reception that follows so they can keep talking about you. Your brother will wish he'd been nicer to you. Your family will be approached by dozens of people who want to share a "you" story but were too shy to speak up at the service. It's a perfect funeral activity because you get the air time you deserve, your family receives the comfort and attention they need, your friends get to feel special, and colleagues and lower-tier friends will wish they'd known you better.

Managing Your Memories

At my funeral, I'll have the officiate(s) provide enough structure to get the crowd into the mood. Then, once the readings are finished, it's pass-the-mic time. In fact, I'm already preparing note cards for various friends so everyone there has at least one all-about-me story to share. They can tell their own stories, too, but in case sorrow fogs their memories, my little scripts will be helpful.

So nobody speaks out of turn, it's a good idea to leave behind a list of topics your friends are forbidden from bringing up. I'm also leaving instructions for my team to interrupt any of my family members, or other guests, if they bring up topics or events from my past that I think should stay dead and buried. It's your funeral; you have the right to control what's said about you. You shouldn't have your dirty laundry aired or embarrassing childhood moments broadcast just because your mother is drunk, or your brother is vindictive, or your crazy friend from high school expresses her grief inappropriately.

I also think it's fair to establish criteria for eulogists, and perhaps even ban certain people from speaking at all. Leaving behind a simple "Thanks For Not Speaking" list is just another way to get the funeral you want and deserve. Remember, you're choreographing a funeral people will be dying to attend. An uninformed guest could muddle your funeral magic. A skilled officiate can manage your wishes tactfully; the banned guest doesn't have to know that, although he's welcome at your service, he needs to keep his pie hole shut. It's your death. You deserve some quality control.

Still, you may want a bouncer and your family liaison on hand. Your funeral bouncer should not be a friend, but an actual bouncer who's paid to do what none of your funeral team members should have to do—remove a disruptive guest from the premises. A friend might not feel comfortable preventing someone on your "do not talk" list from forcing herself into the miclight. It happens. It happened at my friend's church. Right in the middle of a eulogyfest, a drunken man stumbled into the church, grabbed the mic, and carried on for quite some time before he'd had his say. Some people were shocked and upset, some were confused, and others were mildly amused. Only you can decide how much you want to leave to chance.

Start Planning Now

Who do you want guiding the flock? What type of officiate can bring your funeral vision to life? How much *you* do you want in your service?

- Describe your ideal officiate. Include a list of officiates you've approved.

- Make a list of anecdotes and stories for your officiate to use.

- Make a list of eulogies for guests to use, and include a list of approved eulogists.

- Describe any subjects/events/eulogists you do *not* want included in your service or ceremony.

- Assemble a list of bouncers in the area or assign this task to a team member.

- Store information in your funeral box.

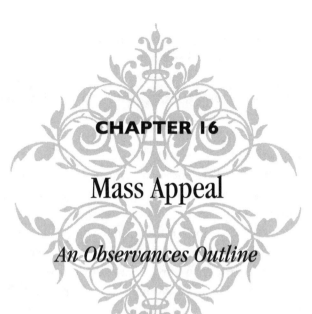

CHAPTER 16

Mass Appeal

An Observances Outline

ven if you have friends in the theater or movie business, or a top-notch officiate who can produce a totally original funeral show for you, it's still a good idea to familiarize yourself with some basic funeral service formats. Why recreate the ceremony wheel? You might find a schedule that, with just a few tweaks, satisfies your aesthetic, spiritual, and celebratory needs.

Sample Schedule

Of course, you don't have to have a "service" if you don't want one. Including some sacred rituals and a few eulogies at your funeral tea, green burial, or commemorative carnival might be all the reverence you want. Either way, reviewing an outline of common service elements may help you organize your chosen remembrance activities. Like any great artist, you have to learn the form before you can break it down and create something new.

The schedule included here is merely a starting point. You

and your funeral team may be envisioning a lineup that's less sedentary . . . or more solemn. Once you get an officiate on board, you can fine-tune the format or change the order of activities to encompass whatever rituals, readings, and performances you choose.

1. Entrance Music

Music is key. It's your first hook, so get it right. Do you want your guests to cry right away or enter the room smiling? Select your entrance song(s) accordingly.

Also, it's time to update this under-utilized element of the service. Walking into a funeral always feels so uncomfortable. Let's change that. Engage your guests from the minute they arrive by including a small interactive activity, or decorations, that will distract them from the gloom and focus their attention on celebrating you *your* way.

Ideas:

- Set the tone right there in the parking lot, or at least in the lobby, by displaying signs and posters bearing your photo, your funeral logo, your death tagline, your favorite quotes, or other images and words that will make your guests feel welcome.
- Don't let tension build before the room fills up. Have guests ring a bell or shout something as they enter. What a release! (Or have an outdoor ceremony so pre-event emotions can dissipate into the air.)
- Have greeters hand out programs at the entrance and stamp each guest's hand (the stamp gets them in to see the cover band and light show after the service). Greeters can also dispense funeral bracelets or other items guests will need during the service, such as candles, kazoos, silk banners, 3-D glasses, flowers, hard hats, and safety goggles.
- Incorporate a small ritual—perhaps your own

funeral hand gesture—that guests can perform as they enter the room and when they sit down and greet the person sitting next to them. (Include an illustration and description in your invitation booklet so guests can arrive prepared.)

  ❧ Ask your team to place little stickers bearing your photo on the back of every seat so your guests will see your smiling face the minute they sit down.

  ❧ Have some class, and use ushers. Late arrivals will especially appreciate some help to their seats.

Sample songs:

As my guests work their way through my end-of-life labyrinth to reach the main ceremony, they'll be accompanied by: "Quiche Lorraine" (the B-52s), "12th Street Rag" (Bob Wills), "Here Comes My Baby" (Cat Stevens), and "I'm Coming Out" (Diana Ross).

If you want your guests to enter crying, try these songs: "Golden Slumbers" (the Beatles), "Blue Eyes Crying in the Rain" (Willie Nelson), "Into the Mystic" (Van Morrison), and "The Sounds of Silence" (Simon and Garfunkel).

2. Welcome

Someone sort of official needs to stand up and let your guests know what they're in for and that they're in good hands.

Ideas:

  ❧ Your designated Death Buddy (your end-of-life equivalent to a best man or maid of honor) can welcome your guests, thank them for coming, and inform them of any special announcements or program changes. This would also be a great time to explain any unfamiliar or physically challenging rituals that will be appearing later in the ceremony.

  ❧ Get it on; bang a gong. Use sound to silence the room and let guests know that the ceremony is about to begin. A rousing bugle call, a soothing pan flute trill, or a clash of cymbals can effectively focus everyone's attention on the front of the venue. Or, "let the games begin" with a starter's pistol or whistle.

• Your officiate or Death Buddy can prevent potentially disruptive guests from interfering with your funeral by asking if anyone has a reason why the ceremony should not proceed as planned. If anyone responds, your funeral bouncer can remove that person immediately. It's a trick, but if it means you get the funeral you want and deserve it's worth it.

I'll be having my officiate ask for a big round of applause—for me. Then, lights dim, fake smoke from stage left, curtain rises . . .

3. Eulogy

It's always a good idea to open your funeral with a story about you. By personalizing your service from the start, you'll help put your guests at ease. A well-crafted introductory anecdote can also be used to set up the reading that follows with special relevance.

On the other hand, following a eulogy with another eulogy (or several) gives your ceremony a casual and inclusive feel since all of your guests, despite their different religious backgrounds, will all be well versed on the subject of *you*.

Ideas:

• Your first eulogist, perhaps your BFF, can recite a list of words that describe you. A list gives eulogists who lack public speaking skills a chance to participate without ruining your service. It can also help an officiate who doesn't know you gain your guests' trust.

• Leave a list in your funeral box if you don't trust your survivors to assemble a compelling compendium. If it's a long list, your officiate can pass it around with a cordless mic so everyone gets a turn

and feels included (without feeling encumbered—
or entitled—to say more).

- Your best friend from college can describe how you two used to stand in the quad, writing spontaneous poetry and handing it out to passersby. She can follow this "so you" story by reading the Aesthetic Manifesto you wrote together after drinking a gallon of cheap wine.

- Your brother can talk about your many runaway attempts as a small child, then segue into few verses by Thich Nat Hahn on "letting go."

- It's always touching when a childhood friend delivers a eulogy. Leave an outline for him in your funeral box so he knows which stories are appropriate to share and which stories are going with you to your grave.

- As a variation on the list-style eulogy, your best friends and family can compile an inventory of your most-used expressions and most adorable idiosyncrasies.

4. Readings

The best readings are brief, easy to understand, and positive. Your readings can be poems, song lyrics, prayers, or excerpts from your favorite books, speeches, movies, and plays. Include at least one reading that everyone can relate to—something philosophical or spiritual that contains a take-home lesson or hopeful message. You probably don't want to have more than three readings because, honestly, they can get boring. For the same reason, you should distribute the readings throughout the ceremony. On the other hand, two back-to-back readings, if they're not too complex, can slow down the pace of your service, allowing the emotional intensity to build.

Selecting your readings in advance helps you effectively express your deepest feelings for your loved ones, promote your most beloved qualities, advance a political or social agenda, protest injustice and greed, or simply entertain your guests. If you don't have friends who can bring your readings to life, assign this task to your officiate or have your team hire an actor or poet.

Ideas:

- Have a sibling read your favorite childhood book or bedtime story.
- Write a love letter to your friends and family that your Death Buddy can read aloud.
- Have your officiate recite a list of books, poetry, and essays you think your guests should read before they die.
- Your reading doesn't have to be read. Your emcee can show a clip from the movie that changed your life.

THE PARTY *of* RON OBVIOUS'S LIFE

RON OBVIOUS
1965–
California, USA

BURIAL ATTIRE: I'm not clear yet on many details of my funeral but I know I will be buried in my green Converse All Star sneakers. I was baptized and confirmed on the same day, wearing green sneakers. I was married in my green sneakers. So, with my exit, I can say that I will have received all the sacraments of my church wearing green sneakers.

5. Music

Your musical selections give your ceremony variety, versatility, veracity, viscosity, and vision. But you need to do more than just have your officiate play your fTunes on the auditorium's sound system. Help your guests get *your* groove thang on by giving them the chance to see, feel, touch, and heal *you*.

Guidelines:

- Always include a visual so your guests don't have to wonder where to look or what to do during the musical portions of the service. Unless there's space for them to get up and dance, give them something to do, like watch a three- to six-minute slideshow of your life. (You can show random photos or have several chronological photo interludes, accompanied by your favorite songs, interspersed throughout the program.)

- Always include the lyrics. Whether your service includes traditional hymns, folk songs, or rock and roll ballads, print the words in the program or display them on a screen in the front of the venue. It's a drag when everyone's singing and you're the only one who doesn't know the words. Also, not everyone likes to sing, so include a short poem or proverb in the program to give non-singers a chance to reflect on their emotions. Sing-alongs can be fun if they fit into the overall theme and energy of the event. Just keep it simple with a well-known favorite, such as "You Are My Sunshine," and add some type of tactile experience, or movement, to get your guests interacting. I'm completely against any ritual involving hand-holding, but having your guest pass around small relics from your life (what else will your family do with the jars of seashells you left in your garage) would give them a little

piece of you. With the right officiate directing the
action, your guests might enjoy clapping or stomp-
ing in unison. It's primal.

- Satisfy your soul and give your guests a new reason
  to rock by hiring a fiddler, accordion player, or a
  bluegrass trio to reinterpret your musical youth.
  While the music's flowing, your guests can file past
  the front of the room so each person can light a
  small candle for you.

6. Ritual

Rituals are important. They help your guests feel like something
sacred is happening. A good ritual gives people a simple way to
connect with each other, feel closer to you, and tap into the universe's cosmic vibrations all at once.

Adding rituals after the less structured elements of your program is an effective way for your officiate to refocus and reinvigo-
rate your guests.

7. Eulogy

Time to talk about you again. With each eulogy you can share
more of yourself, as well as highlight special guests. (Don't forget
my funeral rule of thumb: the more *you*, the more *them*, the more
they pay attention.)

Ideas:

- Write your own eulogy for your officiate or Death
  Buddy to read.
- Write eulogies for your closest friends. Since you'll
  be missing their funerals, why not use part of your
  goodbye to say goodbye to them. Have your team
  or a trusted confidant discreetly slip these eulogies
  into the appropriate gift bags so your most cherished guests have a permanent reminder of your
  love.

> ❧ Leave a long laundry list of commendations and thank-yous for a designated team member to announce.

8. Reading or Ritual

Following a eulogy with the recitation of a beloved poem, a review of the graffiti in the alley by your apartment, or with some other type of a remembrance rite will help your officiate expand on personal anecdotes, making you seem wiser, calmer, edgier, smarter, more artistic, and just "more."

9. Performance

Would you like your service to include a "main event"? That will depend on your funeral goals. If you have several celebratory memorial fêtes in your end-of-life lineup, you may not need or want to include a special performance at your service.

My advice: keep your service nimble with a simple schedule of observances and eulogies, then follow the event with a performance of some sort. Nobody knows what to do after a funeral anyway, so keep the party going. Schedule your service for the late afternoon so you can have a cocktail hour in between functions. You get lots of coverage, and your guests get some spiritual healing and some spirits.

Ideas:

> ❧ Have your friends stage a talent show or create and host a game show of your life.
> ❧ Hire a university professor or two to deliver lectures on your favorite painter, or black holes, or Agalychnis callidryas (the red-eyed tree frog).
> ❧ Rent a movie theater for an evening and have your loved ones screen your favorite flicks or home movies.
> ❧ Keep it low budget. How about a poetry jam, followed by a few hours of bingo?

10. Music

For your third song, you should really go all out.

Ideas:

- ≈ Your boyfriend's band can perform your favorite song.
- ≈ Your three best friends can lead the room in a kara-oke or lip-sync version of your favorite song (these guests should receive a couple of drinks at the en-trance).
- ≈ Make sure every guest has a lighter to hold up in solidarity!
- ≈ Don't forget the accompanying photo tribute.

11. Closing Remarks

It's always helpful to know when a ceremony is ending. There's no need for your officiate to say much; all she has to do is wrap it up with a few words—maybe a parting quote (of yours) or line of verse—and let your guests know what's next in the celebration schedule. You'll definitely want to include a visual: your photo, projected onto a screen for all to see, so your image is clear in your guests' heads as they leave.

12. Departure Music

Always, always end with a song.

Ideas:

- ≈ "I Shall Be Released" (I prefer the Band's version) if you want tears.
- ≈ "Can't Get Used to Losing You" (the Beat) if you'd like to end things on a lighter note.
- ≈ "Praise You" (Fatboy Slim) to pump up the energy and perk up your guests for the next event.
- ≈ "Don't You Forget About Me" (Simple Minds)— message clear.
- ≈ "Stop Your Sobbing" (the Pretenders) if you want

to pull your guests back to reality and remind them to keep on keepin' on.

- ❧ "Wild Horses" (Rolling Stones) will leave your guests in a mellow, nostalgic, weepy mood.

Timing and Other Issues

Nobody likes sitting still for long, so make sure your service is no longer than an hour. Even an hour can be too long if your officiate can't deliver a killer service. If your service includes a "main event," add a 15-minute intermission so people can get up and stretch their legs and visit the restrooms.

On the other hand, if your funeral runs overtime because the eulogies run long or your nephew's KISS cover band plays a few extra songs, that's just fine as long as your guests are enjoying themselves. Lady Bird Johnson's funeral was two hours long. If it's a good show, the time will go by quickly.

Get With The Program

Personalizing your funeral isn't just for you; it's the best way to show your loved ones you care. I've already stored everything my team will need on my iPod (and placed a paper copy in my funeral box). Below, I've listed a few of the readings I've selected for my service. I leave it to my officiates to arrange the various "acts" in an appropriate sequence. I'm trusting you, dear reader, to not rip off my ideas and use them at your own funeral.

- ❧ A recording of Anne Waldman reading "Fast Speaking Woman," probably one of the coolest poems I've ever seen performed.
- ❧ My friend and funeral team member, Sarah, reading "Circe's Power," my other favorite poem, by Louise Glück.
- ❧ My backup CM, Kate, reading sections of *How to Heal the Hurt by Hating* by Anita Liberty. This

book contains one of the funniest break-up letters ever; it's a stellar example of turning pain into art.

ᕦ At least one Shakespeare soliloquy or sonnet.

ᕦ A list of my favorite words, based on how they sound when shouted, what they mean, how they made me laugh when I heard them in movies, and finally, words I made up when existing words didn't adequately describe something or someone. My friend Katie and my backup CM, Kate, will be in charge of assembling my words into a performance and recruiting my funeral team member, Frank, to read them. (I can't reveal any of my "last" words here because I feel I've already told you too much, and I need to keep a few surprises for my guests.)

ᕦ A continuous loop of Paul Rudd and Jason Segel rocking out to Rush in *I Love You, Man*.

I'll be saving the performance, or "main event," for the party of my life. That way, I can pack more eulogies into my service, and keep it simple enough to produce if my survivors end up with several services around the same time. (Sometimes people die in threes. You might want to consider the chance that your guests might have several funerals to attend, or that your team might have other funerals arrange around the same time.)

Start Planning Now

How do you envision the service of your life? Which format gives you the best balance of celebration and veneration? Which readings and rites will entertain and comfort your guests?

ᴥ If you want a service, describe the tone, length, energy, and types of activities you might want to include.

ᴥ Make a list of readings, prayers, chants, blessings, and other observances you want in your service or at other ceremonial or celebratory events.

ᴥ If you don't want a service, describe a few sacred observances your team can incorporate into one of your other funeral festivities.

ᴥ Store information in your funeral box.

"Life does not cease to be funny when people die any more than it ceases to be serious when people laugh."
—George Bernard Shaw (1856–1950), playwright, from *The Doctor's Dilemma*

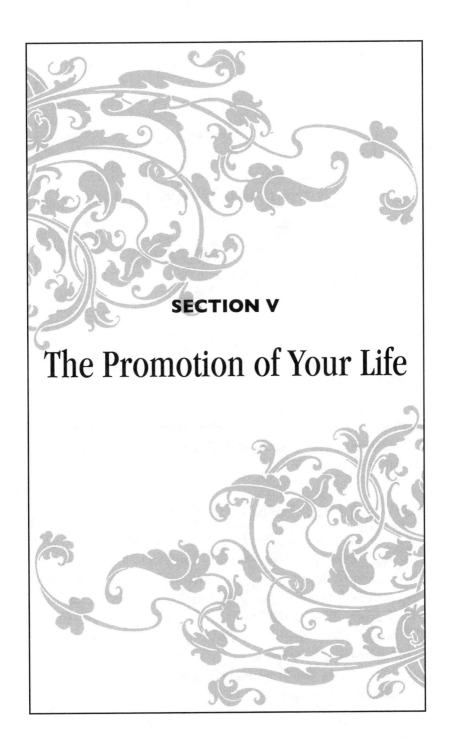

SECTION V

The Promotion of Your Life

CHAPTER 17

Getting the Word Out

Your Funeral ID Card and End-of-Life Announcements

*Q*uick, effective communication is essential in a crisis. It's also the best way to keep your celebration plans on track. That's why you need a death alert system and a competent Notification Master who can quickly contact all interested parties the minute you perish.

First Response: Pocket-Sized Protocol

Too many funerals bomb because, without a clear plan to follow, survivors can lose precious time and focus in the swirl of shock and grief that occurs in the minutes, hours, and days immediately following a death, especially when it's a tragic, untimely death. Your family won't be able to think straight during this period: they won't know where to find the disco ball, how many spinach tofu wraps to order, whether to bury or cremate you, or whom to ban from your funeral. Unless, of course, you have a Funeral ID Card.

This little driver license-sized card, which I invented, is a handy place for you to record basic medical information and the names of your emergency contacts, i.e., your funeral team members. The Funeral ID Card is most useful for accidental, sudden, and public deaths. In these cases, paramedics and police officers will arrive at the scene immediately. They're trained to identify bodies and will search for your wallet. If they find your card, they'll know whom to call about you.

Your Funeral ID card is like the Bat Phone for your death. It will help your team mobilize quickly and get down to the business of taking care of you, body and soul. If your staunchest celebration advocates and Body Boss are notified from the beginning, they can assert your end-of-life plans every step of the way. In other words, they can establish order amidst the hubbub so nobody rushes to honor you before your team has clarified your celebration standards, timeline, and activities. (It's a good idea to list more than one team member on your card, since one of them could be standing next to you when a cement panel falls off the side of a building, instantly crushing both of you.)

Serve and Protect

Your Funeral ID Card isn't just about efficiency. It also serves the important function of protecting your privacy and your family members' feelings, should you die in a compromising situation.

For example, a man in the Pacific Northwest was fatally injured several years ago while having "relations" with a horse. Had he carried a Funeral ID Card, his team members might have been able to keep his equine extracurricular activities secret, protecting his family from the bizarre and painful truth. The story could have been that he died heroically, trying to stop a runaway horse from trampling a small blind child. Sometimes a little editing can do a lot to ease your survivors' pain—one very good reason for listing only friends on your card.

Visit www.thepartyofyourlife.com to download and print a free Funeral ID Card. You might want to laminate it so it'll last longer.

Funeral ID Card of_____

To Whom It May Concern: Please take this seriously! If I am dead, or near death, please contact one of the people listed below immediately, or ask a police officer to do so. Thanks for your help.

Signed: _____ Date:_____

My emergency
contact #1: _____ Phone: _____

My emergency
contact #2: _____ Phone: _____

Please do not proceed with my disposal, funeral, or other death-related activities until contacting these people for instructions. Thanks again! You've helped me get closer to the funeral I want and deserve. Have a nice day.

☐ I am an organ donor. (I am registered with _____ Phone_____)
See the other side of this card for medical information. ➡

Medical Emergency Card

My Name: _____
Address: _____
City/State/Zip: _____
DOB or Dr. License # _____ State: _____
Passport #: _____ Country: _____

Emergency contacts: *see the other side of this card* ➡

My Doctor: _____ Phone: _____
Health Insurance Provider:_____ Plan #: _____
Blood type_____ Medications: _____
My health conditions: _____
Additional Information: _____
My Signature:_____ Date: _____
Witness Signature: _____ Date: _____
Witness Signature: _____ Date: _____
See the other side of this card for vital end-of-life information. ➡

Second Response: Reach Out and Touch Them

Your Notification Master should have the good sense and excellent manners to understand that there's an etiquette involved when dealing with death and mourning. I shouldn't need to say this, but your NM should know that it's not okay to email, text, or tweet about your departure. Forwarding emails and sharing social network posts are easy ways to pass on political petitions, spread good news, and alert friends about the YouTube video du jour, but it's tacky to conduct personal business via computer or cell phone screens.

Call me old-fashioned, but death—especially *your* death—is a big deal and deserves a slower, more personal approach. Even if you like the idea of using an email death notification service, think of your loved ones. Wouldn't they rather hear about their loss from a devoted friend than an impersonal email? They'll have plenty of opportunities to discuss you on Facebook, blog about you, and swap memorial photos *after* the party of your life.

Because your Notification Master loves you, he won't cut corners. He'll take the time to speak with each and every person on your notification list (or at least call the people with three or more stars by their names). Don't waste time setting up a phone tree because someone always drops the ball. If you have a large contact list, your NM can recruit a few friends to come to his home with their cell phones and assist with the initial calls.

You can also rely on a certain amount of word-of-mouth to spread the news. Maybe fourth- and fifth-tier friends will have to read about your departure in the paper. As for work colleagues, your NM really only needs to notify your boss or assistant; either one of them can tell the rest of the office. Ultimately, it's up to you how far you want to reach out once you're gone.

Save the Date

Having a friend contact your loved ones is a thoughtful way to say goodbye to the many people who cared about you. It's also a courteous heads-up for first- and second-tier friends and other potential guests to "save the date" for your life celebration. (It takes time to produce an exceptional life tribute; your funeral does *not* have to happen four or five days after you die.)

One of the bonuses of having a notification list: you can involve a variety of people in your death and set some boundaries around attendance at your funeral at the same time. Not everyone on your notification list will be invited to the party of your life. A skilled NM can politely inform well-wishers that "most likely, the family will be having a small, private ceremony." If individuals ask if there's anything they can do (most people will), your NM can direct them to your funeral website (see Chapter 18), where they can get more information about your public funeral events, make a donation to your favorite charitable organization, and support your loved ones by ordering condolence cards, organic fruit baskets, and other mourning gifts from your funeral gift registry.

THE PARTY *of* SHIRLEY WHITLOCK'S LIFE

SHIRLEY WHITLOCK
1931–
Wisconsin, USA

VIEWS: Planning and thinking about the fun your family is going to have at your funeral is absolutely okay. When you get to be my age, there's nothing to be afraid of. Once you've hit 80, if you've done what you wanted to do—and I certainly have— why not take chances? I don't want to sit and wait to die. I'm tackling piano lessons and my husband is learning the saxophone.

EVENT: I'd like something to be said by a member of the clergy, someone who has a feeling for God as well as a balanced look at things. I want my children to have a wonderful time at my funeral—or whatever they choose to call it—and remember the fun we had when they were young and to

Third Response: Announcement Cards

Once your inner circle has been informed, your NM can send a handwritten note or a printed card to everyone on your notification list. It's a classy way to go.

In the Victorian era, hand-delivered death announcements were a key part of the funeral and mourning process. Having a good death and, more importantly, receiving the proper type and amount of mourning by your community were highly regarded

---

enjoy being there with each other.

DISPOSAL: My husband and I are both going to be cremated. I'd like my ashes spread in the woods and in the lake near our home.

SOUNDTRACK: I can't think of a specific song, but I've been saving bulletins from funerals and marking the music I've liked—a little Frank Sinatra and a little Andrea Bocelli.

RITUAL: At my aunt's funeral they handed out glycine bags containing rosemary sprigs. Rosemary is for remembering. I thought it was a lovely thing to do. If people want to bring something to my funeral, a single long-stemmed rose would be nice, and I think I'd know it if they did.

PLAN B: I have a pact with a childhood friend. If our husbands go before us, we're going to go kayaking in a mangrove forest in Mexico when we're 90, and hold hands and fall out of our kayaks together.

funeral values.

Victorian announcements could be business-card small and simple, or postcard-sized and adorned with illustrations, photographs, poems, and elaborate gold lettering. The best thing about them is that they were cherished mementos of the deceased. With your goodbye card, you'll live on in your friends' memories, as well as in the scrapbooks they'll receive in their funeral gift bags.

You may be tempted to combine your announcement and invitation in one card, but I wouldn't. Each card serves a different purpose, and therefore should have a unique message and style. With two cards you'll gain more exposure and twice the creative options. The announcement card gives your loved ones something to anticipate and buys your team the time to create a funeral schedule that will maximize participation and fulfill your last wishes. Your relatives and closest friends will be comforted by hearing from you (er, your team) during the downtime in between your death and the party of your life.

(Note: you may want to leave separate mailing lists for various notices, invitations, and events. For example, I'm not necessarily inviting the same people to my ash-scattering party as I am to my memorial cabaret. I should also add here that I'm against using www.evite.com to invite people to the party of your life. It's lazy.)

Three-By-Five

A postcard announcement is ideal because it's less expensive to produce and mail than a full-size card and envelope. It's also easier to mount in a memory book or attach to a refrigerator door with a kitchen magnet.

Why not design your card now and save your plans in your funeral box? If you're a fine artist or graphic designer (or have friends who are), you can have a fabulous announcement card that will definitely make your loved ones sit up and take notice. Still, there are many simple options if you're pressed for time or just not very crafty, such as:

- Buy a box of Monet, Van Gogh, or Picasso post-cards and have your team hand-write your announcements (or, if you don't trust your friends to follow through with this task, write them yourself now and have your team fill in the date and addresses after you die).
- If you only have a few friends to notify, make your cards the old-fashioned way with glitter and doilies.
- Leave instructions to have a simple postcard made, bearing your photo on one side and your announcement, funeral logo, and funeral tagline on the other side.
- Have your name printed in black on a white postcard. When you perish, your NM can stamp "canceled" in red ink at an angle across your name, and mail.

Your announcement can be as lavish or as Spartan as you want. If your budget's tight, don't worry. You don't have to have an ornate card to have an elegant card; let the font do the talking. A well-chosen typeface can infuse even the plainest card stock with whimsical energy, nostalgia, and a sense of occasion.

Thanks to Adobe's vast font collection, your funeral card designer will have so many options you might decide to have several announcements for different groups of people on your notification list.

Adobe doesn't have a funeral font category (yet), but they do have a '60s collection. Create a hippy, trippy announcement reminiscent of a Peter Max poster with MOJO or Arnold Böklin. For a cowboy-themed getaway, you might like the WANTED DEAD OR ALIVE font, MESQUITE, something more playful like Giddyup, or a classic Western font, ROSEWOOD, to suggest more of a carnival tone. There are even typefaces for a Roaring '20s-themed funeral or a sci-fi send-off.

Fourth Response: Obituary Options

One of the bonuses of having an invitation-only funeral is that your obituary doesn't have to be so utilitarian anymore. If you're forging your own celebration timeline, breaking free of the traditional four- or five-day funeral turnaround, there won't be a rush to write it, either. Now you can use your obituary to promote your post-life image and entertain your loved ones.

Your friends and family already know most of the mundane details of your life (and the public doesn't need to), so why not make your obituary more interesting? Use it to inspire people to live and die more creatively. Every time I read "She was a devoted wife and mother" in the obituary section of my local paper, I'm overcome with boredom. So beige! *She* was more than that. *She* was a trickster and a poet and a martial artist. *She* never liked olives. *She* danced haikus. In her final days, *she* abandoned her vegan principles and dined on donuts, bacon, and gin. *She* once stole a beret from a sidewalk vendor in Paris while intoxicated. *She* didn't pass away quietly in her sleep, but went out kicking and screaming.

Don't you think your obituary should highlight who you truly were? Remember, every element of your life celebration should have people dying for an invitation (or, post-event, realizing that they weren't invited to the glammest gala of the year). Thanks to online tribute websites, you have many more options than your local newspaper to showcase your life.

Write your own obituary now (there are plenty of helpful websites on the topic) or leave the task to a team member to complete (or hire out). At the very least, write down a basic list of what to include (and what to leave out) so your family has some guidelines. While you're at it, pre-select your obituary photo, too.

You may want to leave behind a few different photos for different publications and uses. If so, make sure you leave very clear instructions about how you want each image used. Your team won't know you want a different photo for your funeral T-shirt than for your funeral program unless you tell them.

Start Planning Now

Make it easy for your survivors to communicate with each other and your public.

🙠 Visit www.thepartyofyourlife.com to print a free Funeral ID Card.

🙠 Make a notification list or at least leave a copy of your address book with your planning materials. Make sure your Notification Master or Mistress knows where to find your lists.

🙠 Design, or leave instructions for, your death announcement card and party of your life invitation.

🙠 Pre-select your obituary and funeral promo photos.

🙠 Visit www.thepartyofyourlife.com for more information about obituaries.

🙠 Store information in your funeral box.

CHAPTER 18

www.yourfuneral.com

Your Official Funeral Website

These days it's essential to have a central source of information about yourself, if not an online presence, in life and in death. Your funeral website will help your funeral team keep your survivors informed about your end-of-life events. It's also an excellent way to live on long after you're gone.

The Memorial Network

A few years ago I was shocked to read about a former classmate's death in my college alumni magazine. Having been just a friend of a friend so many years ago, I hadn't heard about the tragedy that had taken his life more than six months earlier.

Naturally, I turned to Google for more information. I was relieved to find both a blog and a Facebook page with detailed information about him and dozens of photos from his primary memorial service. Thanks to these online resources I was able to contact his family and find out about a local memorial event in my town.

While having a blog, website, or Facebook page is no substitute for memorial events or human contact, it is a simple, quick way for friends (especially your lowest-tier friends, whom you might not invite to your funeral), acquaintances, and loved ones to connect, share memories about you, and stay informed about your funeral festivities.

If you haven't already joined a social networking site, get on Facebook and get back in touch. It's free, and you might be surprised at how affirming it is to reconnect with childhood and college friends. If you want to save money, you could simply have your funeral team convert your Facebook page into your funeral page, but I think you deserve more.

Aesthetically, you can't do much with a Facebook page. So, have your team use your page (or your blog, if you have one) to direct people to your official funeral website. At www.yourfuneral.com, you can really be you with a stylish, professional design (these days, who doesn't have a friend who's a web designer?) featuring gorgeous fonts, engaging graphics, and your favorite (i.e., your funeral) colors. A personal funeral site helps you create your immediate post-life "look," and shows your loved ones that you're serious about the party of your life and they should be, too. (Cost: $10/year for domain name, $150/year for hosting.)

Your Final Domain

You don't have to create your funeral website now, but you might want to develop the basic concepts and describe your design and format ideas, as well as record your preferences for domain names and make a list of potential web designers and hosting plans.

There are benefits to starting early. Reserve a domain name now for the best chance of getting the name you want. You'll also save yourself the hassle of trying to figure it out from your deathbed twenty or thirty years from now. What if you die in your cubicle at work tomorrow? Having your funeral domain locked in will save your team time they can better use tracking down the black and white truffles you want for your black and white funeral banquet.

Early registration will help you establish a site with the

THE PARTY *of* KORD HAMILTON'S LIFE

KORD HAMILTON
1965–
California, USA

FUNERAL:
No organized religion, but I would like attendees to speak. They can say what they want.

PARTY:
I like the Irish wake idea. A huge all-day party, preferably something that people have to travel to (they've gotta do some work—this is going to be a real party!). Maybe my party will be in Mexico, but since most people I know live in San Francisco (where I do), here would be fine, too.

FOOD:
I love Mexican food, so probably a big spread laid out with lots of tequila shots and margaritas.

DRINK:
I can't have just one drink at my party. My favorite is a dry gin martini with olives, served in a *big* glass.

SOUNDTRACK:
Haircut 100, Steely Dan, the Motels, the

cachet of a ".com" suffix. Do you really want to risk ending up as www.you.us or www.you.net? I certainly don't. I'm planning ahead so I get a ".com" death site. Another bonus of setting up your domain name now: the annual price goes down the more years you reserve.

	Romantics, Petula Clark, Eartha Kitt, Annie Lennox, the Carpenters, Cher, Seal, Anita Baker, Blondie, Donna Summer, Chaka Kahn, Deep Forest, Amy Winehouse, and Earth, Wind and Fire.
DISPOSAL:	Cremation. At first I thought I might like my ashes saved, but now I wonder what happens to your ashes when the person you leave them with dies. It seems like an unfair burden to place on someone. And frankly, I don't want an urn containing my ashes turning up at a yard sale.
LEGAL:	I've already assigned a medical power of attorney and completed a medical directive. As half of a domestic partnership, I'm well versed in this.
ENTERTAINMENT:	Would love for someone to read some David Sedaris. I'd like a big screen TV at the party that shows pictures of me and my friends and lovers, as well as death and funeral-related clips from old TV shows, such as *The Dick Van Dyke Show, I Love Lucy, The Mary Tyler Moore Show*, and *Peanuts* (remember the clown episode?).

Establish your site now, and use it to post your yearly news-letter, announce your achievements, publish your travel photos and essays, blog about your favorite topics and celebrity gossip, and even raise money for your funeral fund. For example, if your site qualifies for www.amazon.com's affiliate program, you can add an online store where your readers can purchase anything sold on Amazon, which is almost everything. You'll earn commissions on sales, and your friends and relatives will appreciate the one-stop shopping. Every little bit helps.

Going Live

Once you die, your team can quickly convert www.you.com into an interactive attraction that provides important details about your life celebration(s). Of course, you'll want to save the best content for the months following your funeral events. If people can get all the warm fuzzies they need online, they might be tempted to skip the festivities—especially if they'll have to travel great distances to attend. A few photos and an itinerary are all you need to start.

Maintain the privacy and exclusivity of your farewell gala by having a few password-protected pages. Invited guests will receive the password with their invitations. Your site should include a way for invited guests to contact each other to arrange carpools and to discuss their funeral outfits.

On the public pages, visitors can read your biography and obituary, view photo slideshows and video clips of your life, and find out about your open-to-the-public fêtes. Whenever someone as popular and loved as you dies, friends, neighbors, and colleagues want to do something special in your memory—like establish a scholarship fund, or an annual 5K race, lecture series, or clam bake. A forum or discussion board section on your site would be an excellent place for your survivors to meet and exchange ideas. Depending on how well your survivors understand your sense of humor (or take your demanding personality in stride), why not post a wish list of memorial activities you'd like planned in your honor?

Your site will be a comfort to your survivors. Visitors can sign your online guest book and submit comments and photos. Your family can log in to the site at their leisure.

URL Memorial

Once the festivities have commenced, your Web Master can create your online memorial, adding a slideshow or video of your various end-of-life celebrations, audio clips of the readings, podcasts of your eulogies, and candid interviews with funeral guests.

Many funeral homes now offer webcasts so loved ones who can't attend the funeral service can watch at home. I'm against that. If I have to die, the least my friends and family can do is show up for my party!

By all means, have your funeral videotaped, but keep it a secret. If people know there will be a funeral DVD or webcast available after the event, they might duck out early to attend their kid's soccer game or skip some events entirely.

If you want people to make your funeral a priority, don't give them any option but attending. It's not too much to ask. In fact, even if your team adds your video to your website after the event, they might want to include it in the password-protected area of the site so only invited guests can access it. (Note: there might be a few invitees who are too old, ill, or broke to travel to your service. It's okay to cut them a little slack and give them the password, too.)

The goal of your funeral website is to help you live on so that, long after the party of your life, your survivors can still stay in touch with you and with each other. Don't forget to assign someone to pay the web hosting bill every year for as long as you want the site live.

Your Digital Legacy

Speaking of your online afterlife, how much privacy do you need once you're gone? And whom should be notified about your demise?

You may not care what goes down once you're dead, but what good can come of your next-of-kin accessing your email accounts, cell phone texts, online photo albums, blog, and social networking pages? Find out now what your internet, cell phone, and social networking site providers' guidelines are and make sure you leave instructions for closing these accounts in your funeral box. For example, some email providers require proof of power of attorney, as well as a copy of the death certificate, to release your emails (but they won't disclose your login information). Currently, Facebook and MySpace allow next of kin to remove personal pages or preserve them for memorial purposes, although some features, such as adding or deleting content, may be blocked and viewing access may be restricted to protect your privacy. Twitter has a similar policy. If you're not concerned about privacy, you might want to leave your usernames and passwords in your funeral box so your spouse, Death Buddy, or designated agent can cancel your social networking account(s) or post messages alerting your online friends about your funeral site. (While you're at it, you might want to assign a confidant to get to your house the minute you die and get rid of all your porn or other private items you don't want your family finding.)

What about your online business contacts, gaming buddies, forum friends, and other internet connections? Would you like to let them know when your session has ended for good? If so, there are several web-based end-trepreneurs ready to help you log off of your online life. You can arrange for email death notifications to be sent to a list of contacts you provide when you register; add a photo and obituary if you'd like. Some online notification companies also offer digital storage for email, website, blog, and other web passwords (if you choose this option, you can designate who gets access to this information when you die).

There's also an online death manager service with a safety system that sends you emails on a regular basis, prompting you to respond and confirm that you're still alive. If you've fallen and can't respond, or if you're dead and can't respond, they'll send a notification to your designated access person—a great idea for both business partners and partners in crime. Check out these sites to learn more: www.deathswitch.com, www.slightlymorbid.com, www.legacylocker.com, www.thebelltolls.com, and www.assetlock.net. (Ask your banker and lawyer for advice on the best place to store your financial and other business information.)

Personally, I don't want anyone reading my emails when I'm gone. If my family wants photos of me, stories about me, or to get in touch with my friends, they'll find a CD of approved pictures and anecdotes, as well as a contact list, in my funeral box.

The Death Registry

When you die, so many people will want to honor you and support your family. Make it easy for everyone by including a death gift registry on your funeral website.

Since your registry will be just one of your "last wishes," people will want to accommodate you and, by proxy, your survivors. With a death registry, well-wishers can quickly access and purchase a variety of appropriate sympathy cards, as well as survivor gifts for the recipients you list on your registry, without even leaving their homes. You or your team can pre-select the cards and gift items for the site, as well as provide information on which items have already been purchased (just like a wedding registry), so shoppers will know they're sending original sympathy messages.

As for who makes the survivor gift list . . . I think it should be immediate family and spouses only, unless you have an especially close relationship with a favorite relative or friend. Don't be shy about your death registry, but don't be greedy either. Remember, this is just one request of many you will be making in order to get the funeral you want and deserve. Be creative, but be strategic.

What to Give, What Not to Give

For starters, you might want to make it clear that flowers aren't necessary. Sure, they can be cheerful and decorative, and by all means, have your team incorporate them into the displays and rituals at your end-of-life events. However, as a sympathy gift, flowers have sort of lost their bloom.

Think about it. Would your spouse, domestic partner, or parents really want a house full of flowers? Once a dozen, or several dozen, arrangements start piling up, people can become overwhelmed pretty quickly. Each bright bouquet could become an oppressive reminder of your death. Plus, every flower involved will also wilt, then die, within days. Then your survivors end up with a house full of death. Not good.

Today, many families are requesting donations to the deceased's favorite charity "in lieu of flowers." That's a tidy and thoughtful solution. Still, I think your loved ones need and deserve some special attention and personalized gifts to comfort them during their mourning period.

Maybe your grieving spouse could use a gift certificate to Home Depot so she can finish the garage remodel that came to a halt when you fell off of the ladder and died. Better yet, a weeklong yoga retreat to nurture her body and soul as she adjusts to life without you. What about a trip to Disney World for your kids? You know your husband will fall apart when you depart, so add to your registry wish list that you want someone (preferably one of his buddies and not your hot single neighbor) to take him out to the theater one night while a cleaning crew restores order to his home and a cooking crew fills his freezer with casseroles.

When my friend Cornelia's brother passed away, one of her brother's friends sent her a gift certificate for a local nursery. It was an ideal gift for her because she's an avid gardener. Selecting the plant, designing a place for it in her garden, and planting it were all meditative acts for her. Now, years later, she has a beautiful white hydrangea bush in her backyard, a permanent memorial of her brother. When you set up your registry, you can leave a list of recommended gifts for specific people or a more general list of their interests.

Surviving You Fund

If you're likely to die in poverty or, worse, massively in debt, leaving your family destitute, a nice leather Filofax or iPod Nano isn't going to cut it. Your kids need college funds, and your spouse needs some seed money to start a new business.

You probably didn't think twice about the Williams-Sonoma and Crate & Barrel gifts you registered for when you got married, so don't feel shy about letting your friends know that, for the same amount they paid for that top-of-the-line food processor, they can help get your family back on track.

Instruct your team to add a PayPal button to your site where people can donate money to help cover your funeral costs or pay medical bills. Or set up an account at a funeral fundraising site like www.gofundme,com or www.giveforward.com. (See www.thepartyofyourlife.com for more information on setting up a death registry.)

Start Planning Now

Think about your online life and death. How do you want to use the internet to inform and comfort your survivors?

≈ Write down a list of potential domain names.

≈ If you're ready to start your site now, register your domain name.

≈ Join Facebook and reach out to old friends so you can build up your contact list.

≈ Describe of the type of content you want on your funeral website.

≈ Describe the colors, fonts, and photos you want on your site.

≈ Make an afterlife plan for your online accounts.

≈ Store information in your funeral box.

"All I know is that I'd like to be laid out in a coffin in my own house, right here where I live. I would like my coffin to be put in the double parlor, and I would like all the flowers that are brought to the funeral to be white."

—Anne Rice (1941–), author

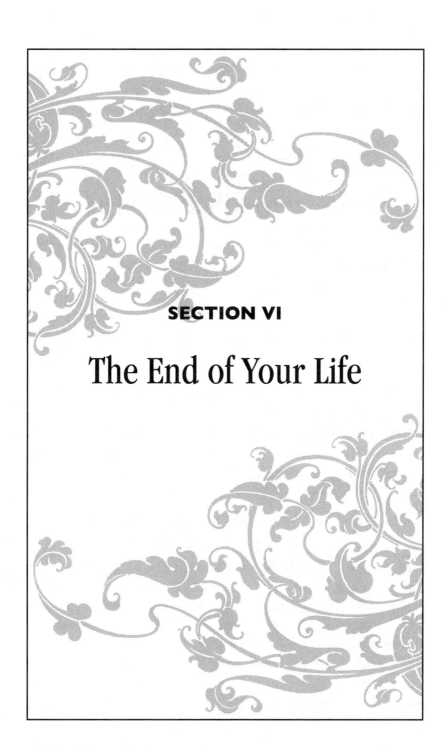

SECTION VI

The End of Your Life

CHAPTER 19

Separation of Body and Party

Establishing Your Celebration Timeline

*I*t's not so simple to just die and get the funeral you want and deserve. Once you stop being you and become a body, you lose control of your party. Worse, your survivors can unwittingly lose control of the death care process if they're not prepared. That's why you need a body plan *and* a party plan.

Time is *Not* on Your Side

The thing is, to pull off a truly funtastic farewell fiesta, your team will need time—time to access the party funds, set up the light show, and weave daisies into the latticework of your funeral gazebo. If you don't have a funeral team and will be relying on a spouse, friend, or family member, that person will need even more time to produce the party of your life.

Your guests will need time, too. They need to start the grieving process, get in touch with each other to reminisce about you and speculate about the guest list, purchase suitable funeral outfits, and shop around for the best airfares to your funeral city.

Unfortunately, when you die, time is not on your side. There are medical, legal, editorial, religious, and commercial systems in place to deal with death—and they get put into motion surprisingly quickly. You may have waited months for that liver transplant, but the minute you die, your body will be processed faster than a FedEx package.

Such a quick turnaround doesn't leave your team adequate time to file the permit for your funeral parade, assemble the string quartet for your funeral tea, or even circulate the "Do Not Invite" list. And you can forget about the ice sculpture in your Bower of Youth exhibit.

Your Body, Your Self

Planning ahead can help you avoid the biggest obstacle to your funeral success: your body. You may not care what happens to it once you're done with it, but your survivors probably will.

It's also likely that they won't agree on how to honor you or on how to dispose of you. Have you forgotten the chaos that delayed some very public funerals? Don't think you're relatives are above some of the dramas acted out by Gary Coleman's and Michael Jackson's families. Consider potential conflicts now so nobody interferes with the party of your life.

You may have your heart set on a certain bejeweled silver urn, but your mother wants you in a titanium casket in the family plot. If you don't speak up now, you could spend eternity shoulder-to-shoulder with your parents and their Yorkie-Poo, Trixie. Meanwhile, your spouse, who has the legal right to decide what happens to you unless you leave other plans behind, wants a natural burial in a wildlife preserve in New Zealand and a memorial ceremony conducted by a *Leaves of Grass*-thumping nudist shaman wannabe. Not a bad plan, but not really *your* dream ending. Plus, in either case, why spend so much money on your body when you're not you anymore?

Prevent hassles later by selecting an exit strategy now. Most states have "personal preference" laws allowing individuals to choose their disposal method and name a designated agent to make their final arrangements. Talk to your lawyer and make your last wishes legal, especially if you want someone other than a spouse or family member calling the shots.

Depending on where you live and die, if you don't leave binding instructions your nutty brother could override your wishes in court. Then you miss out on that sparkly cremains vessel and you'll be too dead to do anything about it.

Don't Hesitate; Separate

You'll have the most planning options, and will buy your team some time if you separate your body from your life celebration(s).

You won't be you anymore, so get out of your own way by creating a death-to-dust itinerary that allows you to make the most out of your demise and your funeral fund. Let your death be its own occasion, complete with it's own observances and soundtrack. Hire a death midwife in advance to help you release your spirit so you can finally power down. Let your team know if you'd like deathbed rites read. Get a ritual all-body cleansing with your favorite all-natural lemon body wash. Your cremation or burial can include festive elements and sacred ceremonies. Just make sure your loved ones know that you want them to slow down the death care process and take the time necessary to plan and stage the party of your life.

With your body plan in hand, your family will be less likely to get sucked into the typical four- or five-day funeral turnaround that people who don't plan their own funerals get. Think of your post-life care as an à la carte menu. You get to pick and choose which services you'd like to use (and when), adapting them to your own needs and timeline.

Take a look around the world to see that there's more than

one way to go:

- In Brazil, it's common for families to hold wakes at home immediately after a death. The deceased is buried the next day, with no ceremony. A week later, there's a service.
- Icelanders have a small, private service a day or two after a death, but the official funeral doesn't take place for a week or two.
- According to Hindu tradition, the deceased's body is usually cremated within 24 hours and a home ceremony occurs after a 10- or 30-day mourning period.
- The Tana Toraja region of Indonesia is famous for its extravagant funeralpalooza pig roasts. Families have a private ceremony following a death, then spend months, sometimes years, planning and saving up for a public funeral festival.

Exit First, Party Later

Direct burial and direct cremation are both excellent ways to divide your demise from your dance party. Selecting either option means that you'll go "directly" from your deathbed to your final resting place without delay or fanfare, giving your team the time it needs to stage your funeral festivities.

A quick exit frees you and your loved ones from the typical funeral schedule. Everyone can say their goodbyes, then take their time grieving. By the time your party rolls around, your survivors will be more stable, more alert, and ready to enjoy celebrating your life. Direct disposal can even be a blessing if you have a slow death. After months of watching you suffer and shrivel, your family and friends might be ready and relieved to efficiently put you to rest. Direct burial and direct cremation are also ideal for people who might be estranged from or live far away from relatives. Cremation only takes a few hours, and direct burial can usually be done within 48 hours of death. Either option is less time-intensive for your survivors than a traditional viewing-fu-neral-reception-burial format.

One of the best things about direct cremation is that you'll be entirely portable, which gives you more post-you life. You'll have so many practical, creative, ceremonial, and even ecological options once you're down to dust. Demand that your ashes be car-ried to Machu Piccu. Attend your own funeral in your new form. Have your ashes turned to art. Cremation isn't a very "green" exit option—it's energy intensive and tosses a lot of pollution into the air—but who knows? Maybe by the time you die, crematoriums will be run on solar or wind power.

Six Feet Under

You can have a direct exit and still give your survivors what they need to feel like they're honoring you in a timely manner.

Direct burial can provide your loved ones with a simple, satisfying, and stimulating way to say goodbye. Nobody really enjoys sitting in a church pew, or even in cushioned auditorium seats, for long. People like to move around, cough, open up pieces of candy wrapped in crinkly plastic, talk to each other, and feel like they're doing something useful. An intimate graveside cer-emony could give your immediate family and first-tier friends the chance to interact with you and each other in a meaningful way. A few words by your emcee, Death Buddy, spouse, or spiritual advisor will give your loved ones just enough ceremony to tide them over until the main event, to be held at a later date.

Green burials are particularly moving occasions because of the natural setting and the opportunities for guest involvement. Imagine your loved ones gathered at a serene, verdant woodland burial ground. With birdsong in the background and the scent of linden trees in the air, your guests will feel soothed and invigorat-ed by your al fresco exit choice. Afterward, your gardening friends can help the staff naturalist replant native flowers and grasses around the site. Natural burial is also an ideal funeral activity for children, who might normally get bored at a typical graveside ceremony. (Remind someone on your team to bring compostable garbage bags for the candy wrappers.)

Don't forget, you can also have a home death, viewing, and funeral, any or all of which give you maximum coverage and your family several days to celebrate you in the comfort and privacy of your own home.

(You may want to have your team videotape all of your post-death activities and include them on your memorial DVD.)

In Between Days: Downtime Diversions

During the downtime between your speedy disposal and your funeral party, your family members and close friends can turn their grief into art by creating a memorial altar, using photos, glitter, ribbons, and your favorite talismans.

Your altar can be decorative or functional, or both. Displaying altars and making offerings to altars are both common funeral rites in Buddhist and Hindu traditions. Making altars is also a popular celebration activity during Dia de los Muertos festivals around the world. Assembling your altar will give your loved ones something to do in the days immediately following your demise, providing them with an outlet for their grief, as well as a small sense of occasion.

Once your altar is on display, your family can host a body-free wake or other ceremony. If you're cremated, have them add your urn to your altar; decorating your urn can be part of the ritual. Your guests can chant, pray, sing, and interact with your altar as a daily vigil that continues until your official memorial service or the party of your life. Depending on your event schedule and spiritual needs, you might want more than one altar: a private one for your home, a public one for your Memory Room, and one at your grave—for you.

Sample Celebration Timelines

Here are a few sample celebration timeliness I created to give you an idea of how you can have an efficient exit and a fantastic farewell party.

The Untimely Demise
- You are fatally trampled while attempting to run with the bulls in Pamplona.
- Have your body repatriated and flown home to your loved ones. (Good travel insurance will include a return flight for your boxed self.) A cheaper option: get cremated in Spain and mailed home. A more festive option: have your inner circle fly to Spain and bury you there. Or they can hike into the Pyrenees to scatter your ashes.
- If you choose repatriation, your stateside burial can be taken care of quickly. Afterward, a happy hour reception where people can stop by for some sangria and paella.
- Party of Your Life TBA. A month after your demise, everyone can gather for your life celebration, which will feature a flamenco dance performance.

Your Time Is Up
- You die after a long battle with a fatal illness at age 65.
- You're not attached to your body. Your cremation preference is immediately implemented, without fanfare, as you wished.
- Your ashes are stored in the cardboard container from the crematorium for a few weeks while your funeral team tries to find a time to meet and put your party plans into action.

- Your three best friends are dispatched to scatter most of your ashes at three secret locations.
- Your spouse commissions a local artist to paint your portrait, using paint with a dash of your ashes mixed in.
- Two months after your death, friends and family rent out an old movie theater and watch *The Seventh Seal* and *Ran*, your two favorite movies. After the screenings there are drinks, discussions, a few eulogies, then drinks and poker until dawn.

The Natural Way

- You perish peacefully in your own bed after a long, productive life.
- Your death midwife arrives to bathe you and dress you in your favorite outfit (or better, in an elegant, cozy, handmade felt shroud).
- Your family hosts a home visitation. You rest on dry ice while your guests mingle, say goodbye to you, nibble on canapés, and look through all of your old photo albums, your record collection, and other memorabilia.
- The next day you are transported to a green burial ground and wildlife preserve where your best friend reads your favorite poem to you before you are interred in your shroud, surrounded by friends and family.
- Your niece records the GPS coordinates of your green burial plot so future visitors can find you easily.

(See Chapter 21 for more on home-based funerals.)

Timing is Everything

Give your team at least a month, if not six to eight weeks, to orchestrate your life celebration plans once your body plan has been executed.

Even if the party of your life will be small and easy to organize, you'll want to give your out-of-town guests at least the 21-day advance they'll need to find the best airfares. (If they get stuck with exorbitant fares, there's a chance they won't come at all, but instead send an attractive floral arrangement in your honor.) If most of your favorite people live in another state or country, why not hold your main ceremony or celebration where they live? Since you're going to separate your body from your party, you don't need to be there. Reduce the carbon footprint of your death and select a location that maximizes attendance and

---

THE PARTY *of* DAN DILLMAN'S LIFE

DAN DILLMAN
1934–
Illinois, USA

VIEWS:	I don't want a mourning, but a celebration of life—a party.
EVENT:	A gathering of family and friends to remember and talk about the good times.
FOOD:	There should be plenty of my favorite food on hand (Reuben sandwiches, meatloaf, shrimp cocktail, and baklava) and drinks to fuel the participants.

minimizes travel for all.

Set a deadline for your memorial bash so that it's not post-poned for longer than six months, after which time people may have moved on and be less interested in attending.

If You Do Nothing

Your fancy plans notwithstanding, when the time comes your family might not feel comfortable departing from the conventional funeral timeline and protocols. That's why it's worth repeating—discuss your plans often and assign a designated agent who won't let anything or anyone derail your one-of-kind funeral line-up.

Even if your loved ones know about your plans, they might

DRINKS:	Maker's Mark Bourbon, Dos Equis, Negra Modelo, and Smithwick's.
SOUNDTRACK:	An eclectic selection of music from classics, blues, country, jazz, and swing—especially music from the '30s and '40s. If Alison Krauss and Dr. John could stop by for a couple of sets, that would be very cool.
DISPOSAL:	Cremation.
RITUAL:	Before my ashes are sent off to the University of Michigan to be scattered along the Diag and at the Big House, they (I) need an appropriate send-off. All attendees should face Ann Arbor and sing several rousing choruses of "The Victors"!

feel pressured to get you into "the system." That means they'll start feeling rushed, and there goes your death to-do list. They might remember to retrieve your hand-embroidered silk burial shroud from storage, but fat chance that they'll be able to hire your favorite calligrapher to inscribe the invitations on such short notice because she has a month-long waiting list. Suddenly, your team will start to feel like they're trying to fit a rectangular casket into a round hole. It's inevitable that they'll feel like they have to cut corners to make their (your) deadline.

Worst case scenario—your body will be processed so quickly that your team could lose their resolve and decide to have your funeral right there and then at the funeral home because . . . well, there you are, all boxed (or urned) up and ready to go. Then your hard work goes down the drain like so much toxic embalming fluid. No disco ball, no chocolate hazelnut funeral biscotti, no organic shea butter hair pomade in the gift bags. And your college friends won't be there because in the rush, nobody remembered to call them.

Don't let this happen to you, and don't leave your family feeling boxed in by the traditional funeral schedule. Define your body plan, and create your own celebration timeline. The fewer obstacles your team has to overcome, the closer you are to achieving your funeral goals.

Start Planning Now

Don't let your body get in the way of your special day. Think about your death to dust itinerary, and:

❧ Select a disposal method. Consult a lawyer about assigning a designated agent to take care of your disposal.

❧ Write down your ideal end-of-life disposal and celebration timelines.

❧ Make a list of any permits, certificates, applications, or other forms that your team will need to complete to produce your funeral, the party of your life, and related events. (Visit www.thepartyofyourlife.com for more info.)

❧ Give your survivors clear instructions that it's okay to break with tradition—it's what you want.

❧ Store information in your funeral box.

CHAPTER 20

To View, Or Not to View

How Do You Say Goodbye?

While you're breaking down your farewell into manageable celebration events, you might want to consider breaking free from two common funeral traditions: the viewing and the open casket funeral. Both practices may lock you into the conventional death care system and the quickie funeral. Plus, they're just not very festive.

Keep a Lid on It

From a creative, aesthetic, and entertainment perspective, open casket events are a drag. Who wants to look at a dead body, much less a stiff, plastic facsimile of the fancy flower you used to be? "Restored" corpses give me the willies. They're phony, weird, and depressing. It's not the real you. Getting all made up to look like you're just fine, like you're "at peace," is like a complete denial of all the hard work you put into dying. It's like your character and personal style and blemishes have been glossed over—for what, and for whose benefit? Plus, do you really want people lining up to gawk at you when you're at your worst?

What if your nemesis manages to slip past the bouncer and sneaks a peek at you—and pities you? Worse, the guy you've been pining for over the past two years could see you with your airbrushed face and shellacked hair and think, "Oh, I thought she was cuter." Don't kid yourself; just because you're dead doesn't mean people stop judging you. It's better to control your image until the bitter end than give people opportunities to imprint in their memories new, less flattering pictures and thoughts of you.

Personally, I don't want anyone looking at me when I'm dead, unless I'm freshly dead. And even then, only my inner circle gets to see me. Hopefully, I won't be naked, but wearing my favorite organic cotton skinny jeans, a slimming, black merino wool top, my elegant, hand-tooled silver hoop earrings, and my ass-kicking motorcycle boots.

If my people want a last look, they'll have to deal with the real, dead me, not some sanitized, waxen version of me. They have to stare my death in the face—my face. Example scenario: my lover, standing above my crumpled body at the intersection of 2nd and Pine after a Metro bus driver, high on decongestants and Vicodin, has run over me in the crosswalk. That's real. It's also cinematic. Or my niece and nephew, sitting at my bedside on my 102nd birthday as I drift into The Big Sleep. That's natural.

Wake Me Up Before You Go Go

Let your guests off the hook. They really don't want to see you all stiff and waxed out. They'll attend your end-of-life events to honor and celebrate you, not to actually see you. They don't need a casket or a body in front of them to get in touch with their love for you. Your presence will be felt everywhere—in the photos in your Memory Room, in the sweet stylings of Nina

Simone swirling out of the speakers at the farewell service, and in the fancy velvet dinner napkins you insisted your team order for your funeral banquet.

By skipping a viewing, you don't have to miss out on having a pre-funeral event. Go ahead and have one, just don't be there. A visitation is really about the visiting, anyway. Better yet, have a "wake up," a kick-off party designed to celebrate your life and encourage your survivors to be happy that *they* are still alive. Your team can post a freestanding, life-sized photo of you at the door. Your guests can play Trivial Pursuit-type parlor games based on

---

THE PARTY *of* PHIL ZRIMSEK'S LIFE

PHIL ZRIMSEK
1965–
Minnesota, USA

VIEWS:	My biggest fear is that I'd plan this elaborate funeral and then no one would show up. It would be very embarrassing. So I'm thinking bare-bones minimum.
EVENT:	No visitation. I don't want people looking at me. I don't want a funeral. If my survivors want to have an informal memorial party and have a few beers and some wine, that's okay.
ORGAN DONATION:	I'll donate my organs, but I don't want my body donated to science. I don't want a bunch of med students giving me

your life. Create a light, celebratory atmosphere with party hats, fruit plates, and uplifting but classy music.

If you're dead set on a viewing, then have a home visitation. That's both real and natural. It's more honest, really. What better way for your loved ones to get in touch with your death than to see you looking dead? As you'll read in Chapter 21, it's the true American tradition. Home viewings are also economical. No restorative arts and, since you'll be laid out in your own bed or on a table, you won't need a casket. (If you want a viewing casket, your family can rent one by the hour.)

---

	a funny name and messing around with my body.
DISPOSAL:	I don't want to put anybody out. I just want my body done away with and no hassles. I want the cheapest cremation possible (definitely the cardboard cremation casket), and my survivors can toss the ashes and body fragments in a hole in the backyard.
LEGAL:	I'm considering adding a provision in my will that my estate will pay for a keg at my college class reunion. The Zrim keg. And I want all of my clothing and household goods donated to charity; an auctioneer can sell off the rest of the stuff and donate the money to charity. I don't want my relatives descending on my house and pawing through my stuff.

If You Do Nothing

In their grief, your survivors will likely turn to a funeral director for guidance. If they do, they may be asked if they'd like a viewing and an open casket funeral.

If your family wants a viewing, thinking it's the best way to proceed, they might be told that you must be embalmed first. This isn't true, of course, unless you die in Minnesota, the only state that requires embalming for viewings, but your survivors won't know that. They also won't know that they can have a viewing without a casket.

For too long, people have accepted the idea that it's better to see a corpse that's been restored to look not so dead than to deal with the reality of a dead-looking corpse. (Also, people have been lazy and haven't pre-planned their deaths.) They might think differently, and I hope you will, if they know what happens on the mortician's table. Embalming is an incredibly invasive, gruesome procedure. (I'll be discussing this topic, along with other death-related issues, in my next book, tentatively titled *The End of Your Life: Get the Death You Want by Planning It Yourself*. For now, you can read a compelling case against embalming in *The American Way of Death Revisited* by Jessica Mitford.)

Remember, your loved ones may not be thinking clearly in the hours and days following your departure. That's why you need to understand your options so you can help your survivors make the best decisions for *you*.

More Than This

Your viewing choice is also a matter of resource allocation. Do you want your hard-earned funeral funds going into a casket, embalming, and "restorative arts," or hanging from the ceiling in the form of a great big sparkling disco ball at your funeral disco?

By not frittering away your money on a viewing, you'll have at least $3,400 (the average amount survivors pay for a casket, plus the cost of embalming, restorative arts, and room rental) in your party fund for other, more important purchases. That's enough for 100 decks of playing cards imprinted with your funeral logo or a photo of you ($375), a *Star Trek* Cemetery Headstone Marker ($225), nine bottles of gin ($250), 10 trays of spring rolls, potstickers, and chicken satays ($450), burial of your ashes at a Florida nature preserve burial ground ($200), karaoke machine rental ($100), a funeral piñata ($12 basic or $25 Batman) filled with fair trade chocolate bites ($25), ceremonial slippers for funeral team members ($100), a five-layer funeral cake ($700), a 14-karat-gold Buddha ash pendant for your Death Buddy ($300), and iPads for your co-Celebration Masters ($1,000).

Start Planning Now

Considering your privacy concerns, aesthetic standards, and funeral budget, how do you feel about people looking at you when you're dead? How do you think they'll feel about looking at you when you're dead?

🙠 Declare your viewing views.

🙠 Store information in your funeral box.

CHAPTER 21

Take Back Your Death

Home Deaths and Funerals

*I*f you're looking for another way to personalize your passing, not to mention slow down the funeral process and save some money, consider staying at home. Home viewings and funerals offer your loved ones a meaningful way to honor you that they can manage at their own pace.

The Modern Funeral

In your lifetime, funeral homes have been the de facto choice when there's a death in the family. It's where people go, and it's where survivors are referred to by hospitals. Funeral directors and morticians are trained and licensed to care for your body, and funeral homes pretty much provide one-stop shopping for all of your death care needs.

They take care of transportation, complete and file the necessary paperwork, prepare the body for viewing and disposal, make funeral arrangements, sell caskets and urns, and arrange for burial or cremation. Plus, they're networked with cemeteries, crematoriums, and members of the clergy, so it's a pretty straightforward and organized system.

It wasn't always this way. Not so long ago families cared for their own dead, as was the custom in many cultures around the world. It wasn't until the American Civil War that many of the common practices we consider "traditions" began.

Death: A Family Affair

Death used to be so simple (and affordable). You died at home, and your family sent word to the local carpenter or cabinetmaker to build you a casket. Meanwhile, the women (i.e. family members, or, if your family had money, nurses or midwives), cleansed your body, wrapped you in a sheet or gown, and laid you out for viewing in the parlor. Someone sat with your body overnight (to make sure you were really dead, among other reasons) and friends and relatives stopped by to see you. Then your family had a simple funeral and buried you on their property or in a cemetery. There's a good chance your survivors dug your grave themselves. In other words, your people were intimately involved with your death.

When Civil War casualties started piling up, everything changed. Long story short, transporting slain soldiers back to their families before their bodies putrefied created the need for some type of short-term preservation. Doctors created a toxic cocktail of chemicals, including arsenic, to embalm the bodies, and trained undertakers to perform the process. Out of this gruesome battlefield scenario, an industry was born and thousands of grieving families were spared from seeing their loved ones in a horrific state of decay. Embalming became more popular despite the commonly held belief by Christian Americans that it was a pagan death rite. Even Abraham Lincoln was embalmed, and he looked so good on his cross-country train tour that people started to accept the practice as a necessary custom.

The sad thing is that, over time, from generation to generation, we've lost touch with the personal experience of death. Strangers care for our dead now, and death has become sanitized, organized, and removed from our daily lives (not to mention, very expensive). All we have to do is show up at the funeral and follow along. We're so removed from the process that death and dead bodies seem scary and morbid rather than a natural part of the life cycle. We pay people to make the deceased look less dead, which isn't natural at all. We're missing out on a meaningful, necessary rite of passage by not fully participating in end-of-life care.

THE PARTY OF THOM HASLITT'S LIFE

THOM HASLITT
1980–
Paris, France

THEME:
There should be a theme; every good party has a theme. I want my guests to dress up as their favorite dead people.

DRINK:
Cosmos, and for once I won't be stuck behind the bar making them all night!

VIEWS:
People should have some time between my death and my party to get over their boohoos. I want my friends and family to remember the fun times, the challenging times, and to drum up some new drama in the process.

Bringing It All Back Home: The DIY Goodbye

Wouldn't it be nice to bring your family back into the fold? Give them the opportunity to truly experience your death? What about you? Wouldn't you like to die in the comfort of your own bed, with your spouse lying next to you as you draw your last breath, or with your loved ones gathered in the next room, listening to your favorite albums? And for once, wouldn't it be nice to have a family gathering at a location that's convenient for *you*? It's all possible if you plan ahead. Why not revive antebellum customs, and take back your death?

EVENTS:	My goodbye will be like a scavenger hunt that takes my friend and family to my favorite locations: a restaurant in Paris, a vineyard in Oregon, and a steaming volcano in Costa Rica. (I might even plan a detour to my favorite grocery store for a jar of mustard or two!) The party will end with a trip to my burial plot in Wisconsin.
BODY PLANS:	No embalming. No viewing the corpse (unless you are into that sort of thing—and then *no* photos!).
PLAN B:	If I'm killed in a tragic accident and my survivors receive a huge settlement, then I want a three-week, 'round the globe, all-expenses-paid vacation for my closest friends. Then I will find out who my diehard friends are—who would be willing to take off three weeks from work for me?

Just as more people are choosing home births, there's a growing interest in home deaths. Your family can DIY it, use the hospice care system, and get help from a variety of end-of-life providers, such as home funeral guides and death midwives, so that you can spend your final days at home. For the price, convenience, and spiritual benefits, who wouldn't want a more natural, private exit? Your passing can be an event in itself or easily segue into a home viewing or visitation (or "wake"), followed by a home funeral. Depending on where you live, you can even be buried at home. Plus, your team can still stage the party of your life at a later date.

Lay Me Down: Home Vigils and Wakes

Die at home, and you can ditch the body bag. Instead, you'll be lovingly cleansed by a loved one or death midwife, then anointed with aromatic essential oils. You'll be gently swaddled in your favorite high-thread-count organic cotton sheets, laid to rest on your antique, hand-carved teak daybed from Bali, and allowed to take your own sweet time just being dead for a few days before your disposal. Who wouldn't want a final spa day?

Home death vigils and visitations give your family quality time with you in a relaxed, familiar environment. They can participate as they wish, have more control over the process, and not feel rushed. I spoke to several home funeral guides during my research who explained that family members and friends innately know what to do in these situations because an organic rhythm and energy arises that helps people settle into a slower pace and find acceptance.

Your all-natural downtime could be like an extended open house or wake that takes place over an afternoon or a couple of days, with friends stopping by to spend time with you and with each other, children picking wildflowers for your room, and your best friend making vats of chicken noodle soup for your guests. It's all legal, safe, and affordable. You won't smell or rot in those few days because you'll be resting on dry ice.

Your house can be transformed into a memorial gallery, with each room showcasing your achievements and passions. Your friends will enjoy seeing all of your fly-fishing gear on display. Your young nieces and nephews will get a kick out of your electric guitar collection. Your team can clean house, too, by giving away your books, art, and ski equipment as parting gifts!

What better way for your survivors to face death and move through grief than a hands-on participation in the end of your life?

Who Cares?
Selecting End-of-Life and Post-Life Providers

If you like the idea of returning to a more natural, more afford-able way of death, you're not alone (nor will your family be). Home funeral guides and death midwives are the new go-to death care providers, dedicated to helping you take back your death.

Since home funeral guides and death midwives aren't cur-rently licensed or regulated by individual states, as funeral directors are, their experience, training, and services may vary. In general, both types of death care providers help families care for their own dead at home. Here's a breakdown of typical services you might expect from death midwives and home funeral guides:

> ❧ *Death midwives* provide support for the dying and their family. Some offer body care and family sup-port; others work on a more spiritual and emo-tional level, supporting you through the death pro-cess. Sometimes called "death doulas," death mid-wives may use massage, music, or other modalities to help you wind down and let go. Some midwives come from a clergy or nursing background. There are a variety of death midwives out there to suit your personal death style—maybe you'd like a

pagan midwife? Or a spiritual death midwife? Or just a regular death midwife?

ॐ *Home funeral guides* provide education, guidance, and support for families wishing to plan a home vigil or funeral. Their main role is guiding families through the home funeral process, assisting them as a funeral director would. Home funeral guides are also called home funeral facilitators or home funeral consultants. (Others, who might refer to themselves as home funeral educators, provide information and training for families, but may not get involved with home funeral services.) It's common for home funeral guides to have a nursing or clergy background. Some are also licensed funeral directors.

Compared to the number of funeral directors in this country, the new death care providers are small in numbers, but their posse is growing. In 2010, several of the leading home funeral advocates and educators formed the National Home Funeral Alliance (www.homefuneralalliance.org). Their mission: to educate consumers about home-based funerals, minimally-invasive and environmentally-friendly death care, and green burial. (See list of providers in the Party of Your Life Resources section, page 254.)

You and your family may want or need to coordinate your end-of-life and immediate post-life services among two or more providers. For example, your death midwife might be the person for your post-death care, and she might have a great shroud contact for you, but your local funeral home might be the handiest provider for your post-life transportation needs. Both death midwives and home funeral guides work with funeral directors to help families cover all the bases.

Funeral directors can also help you plan a home farewell. Now that home vigils and family-directed funerals have become more popular, funeral homes are adapting their services to meet demand. In fact, the National Funeral Directors Association now offers a home funeral web seminar for funeral directors, taught by a home funeral guide. Bottom line: shop around until you find the provider that fits your needs.

(Note: whomever you select to handle your after-life care, it's always a good idea to check credentials and licensing [where required], as well as ask detailed questions about an individual's services and experience. It's even okay to ask for references. In some cases past clients might be willing to provide them. Just keep your inquiries brief and respectful. See www.thepartyofyour-life.com for the types of questions you can ask when "interviewing" a potential death care provider or her references.)

Paperwork, Permits, and Providers

The best way to involve your loved ones in your home-based exit is learning more about your options now. If they're not in it from the start, they probably won't follow through once you're gone.

Most people don't know that it's perfectly legal to care for their loved ones, as well as prepare them for their final journey, at home. (Even if you die in a hospital or nursing home, you can still come home for a few days before your final disposal.) Death isn't actually that complicated or mysterious, and in many states, your family may not need to work with a funeral home at all.

Why not take a class on home death care or memorial planning with your family? That's quality "together" time, and even if you plan on living another twenty or thirty years, you can put your knowledge to use by helping others plan their home funerals until it's your turn. (See www.thepartyofyourlife.com for links to home funeral resources.)

If your friends and family are hardcore DIYers, they may

want to manage your home vigil, visitation, and funeral them-selves. All they have to do is follow state laws and make sure they complete the required paperwork in a timely matter. Filing fees are minimal—usually less than $20, and in some cases, free. (By the way, a true friend would be willing to put you in his biodeisel van and drive you to your natural burial plot himself, freeing up a few hundred dollars that might be better spent on a plane ticket for a down-on-his-luck friend to attend the party of your life.)

Check these sources for information on your state's funeral laws and compliance requirements:

- The Funeral Consumers Alliance is a nonprofit or-ganization dedicated to protecting the rights of fu-neral consumers. The FCA website (www.funerals.org) contains many useful planning tips and arti-cles, money-saving advice, updates on state funeral laws, and links to state organizations that provide information on planning home funerals.
- *Caring for the Dead*, written by Lisa Carlson, exec-utive director of the Funeral Ethics Organization (www.funeralethics.org), is a state-by-state guide to funeral, burial, and cemetery laws.

In the end (your end), give your family the chance to care for you and save some money by hosting your own death.

Start Planning Now

Wouldn't you like a final sponge bath with your favorite organic rosemary body wash . . . not to mention the convenience of just staying in for your funeral?

ᔍ Describe your ideal home funeral schedule.

ᔍ Visit www.thepartyofyourlife.com for links to home funeral resources.

ᔍ Research funeral homes, home funeral guides, death midwives, and green burial grounds in your area.

ᔍ Store information in your funeral box.

CHAPTER 22

Plan B

When There Is No Body

*I*n these uncertain times, it's wise to let your survivors know how you'd like them to proceed if you go missing and are likely to be dead.

It Could Happen to You

Don't kid yourself. People disappear all the time. Pirates have made a big comeback, at least in some parts of the world. Kidnapping is still very popular in other parts of the world. People fall overboard during fantasy cruises or while working on fishing boats. They perish in avalanches. They climb the highest peaks and never return. They fly or float over an ocean or an inhospitable desert, and fall off the radar. Poof. Gone.

Even if you're not the adventurous type, you could perish in a crash, a fire, or worse, leaving your loved ones without a body or enough evidence to determine if you are simply missing rather than dead. Your survivors, especially if you have a spouse, need to know what to do if you drop out of sight or are "missing and presumed dead."

Hope for the Best

Considering the many possibilities, how long would you like your survivors to keep up the search? If you get lost on a hike, you could probably survive in the woods for a week or two if it's not too cold. You might survive a plane crash in a remote jungle, but not be able to find your way back to civilization. Do your survivors have the resources to keep up the search once the rescue pros call it off?

If you're famous or rich or both, you have a better chance of keeping the search and rescue teams going. The U.S. Coast Guard searched for Japanese balloonist Michio Kanda for 16 days when he vanished while attempting a solo flight across the Pacific Ocean. He was never found. Aviator and adventurer Steve Fosset disappeared in September 2007, and a year later, his friends started a new search for his remains. His widow paid more than $2.6 million dollars on private and state agency searches. Thirteen months after he disappeared, hikers found his wallet, which helped officials find the crash site and his remains.

The thing is, you have to consider the pain your family and friends will endure every day that you're not found. They need closure, and if you have a family, they probably need access to your life insurance benefits. (Fosset's wife waited three months before petitioning a court to pronounce her husband legally dead.) Give them a break and leave behind a few likely "missing" scenarios and a time limit for searches.

The only silver lining to your untimely disappearance: your survivors will have plenty of time to realize your funeral vision. No body, no rush. They'll also save money—no burial, no casket, no urn. All of your funeral funds can be funneled into the party of your life.

Baby Come Back

Depending on your lifestyle and your business associates, you might want to consider a payout plan that keeps some of your assets in an untouchable account for a few months after your death. That way, if you're missing and declared dead, but in real-

---

THE PARTY *of* CHET HAASE'S LIFE

CHET HAASE
1965–
California, USA

VIEWS: I honestly haven't ever given my funeral any thought because, well, I won't even get to enjoy it. What a pisser. After a lifetime of feeling like there were a myriad of parties that I never get invited to, here's the one party that, by definition, is by and for me. And I'll have to pass. Plus, I don't even like organizing things that I get to take part in; why would I waste my effort organizing something that wouldn't benefit me at all?

DISPOSAL: I would rather be cremated than take up more precious land resources just so my family could feel guilty every holiday about not hauling themselves out to the graveyard to see Dad's plot. Just burn me, scatter me, and be done with it. No guilt; just a little bit of Chet mixed in with the rest of the particles in the universe.

ity you've been hexed by a sorceress who's holding you captive on an unknown island, or shipwrecked in Borneo and suffering from amnesia, there will be some money left in your accounts when you finally make it home and resume your life.

On a similar note, if you have a secret or double life, it might be a good idea to keep a detailed journal. Maybe you're exactly the type of person to go missing. Your diary might help the police find you.

Don't worry about how awkward it might be if you make it back alive after you're presumed dead and your team has already produced your super send-off. No harm done. Everyone (except your family if they find out you have another family) will be so happy to see you that they'll get over the fact they just mourned your death. They'll probably throw a huge party in your honor. Another bonus: you'll get to watch your funeral video and see who really came through for you in the end.

Your Money or Your Life

In case you're tempted to pull a Huck Finn and show up at your own funeral, or worse, fake your death for the purpose of throwing your own funeral, don't do it. Sure, it would be wonderful to see how people really feel about you, but your loved ones will not appreciate being tricked into grief and mourning, not to mention purchasing a park bench in your memory, no matter how good the gin is.

One of my friends knew a man who pulled such a funeral scam, and all he accomplished was pissing off the people who cared about him the most. It's just bad business. You'll end up without any friends, and, when the time comes, you will have already exhausted their funeral goodwill. When your number is really up, how will your guests truly let go and celebrate you if they're wondering whether you're playing a joke on them? Don't be greedy, and don't waste your dramatic edge on a faux farewell.

It should go without saying—it's totally lame to fake your

death and try to collect your insurance money to start a new life in some remote location. A British couple tried this and got caught. Instead of using their insurance bounty to get out of debt, they ended up with six-year prison sentences. Crime doesn't pay. If you have money problems, maybe bankruptcy is an answer. Then you can still have a good funeral when the time comes.

Start Planning Now

You never know what could happen to you. Save your survivors some time and pain by describing a few "missing and presumed dead" scenarios.

❧ Decide on a rescue timeline that allows your survivors to let go after a reasonable amount of time.

❧ Don't be so quick to give away your assets. Talk to your lawyer about the best way to structure your will.

❧ Store information in your funeral box.

" . . . I've a great fancy to see my own funeral afore I die."
—MARIA EDGEWORTH (1767–1849),
novelist, from *Castle Rackrent*

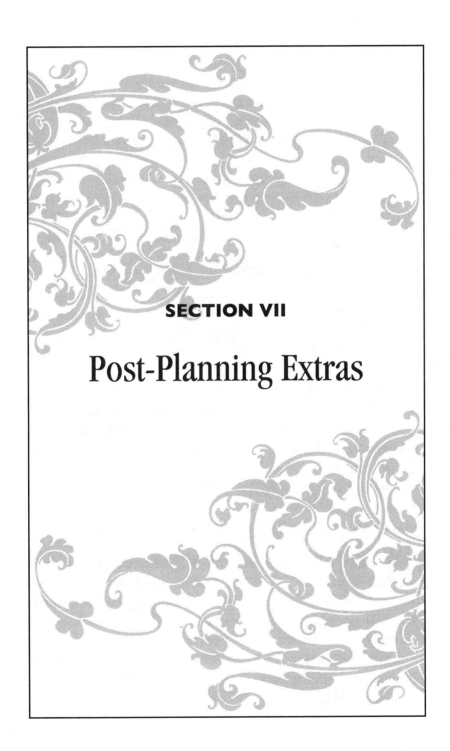

SECTION VII

Post-Planning Extras

CHAPTER 23

Financing the Fun

Need-to-Know Shopping Info

*E*ven though the focus of this book is the party of your life, you may want to start considering end-of-life planning, too (i.e., purchasing death merch and services), so you can create a comprehensive funeral budget. I'd like to leave you with some basic information about your rights as a funeral consumer, as well as a few ideas on financing the fun!

The High Cost of Dying: The Buck Stops Here

Selecting party streamers and strobe lights is easy, but when it comes to your final disposal, your team will need help. Consumers purchasing funeral services are uniquely vulnerable customers: they're exhausted and overwhelmed with emotions, they don't really know what they need or how much products and services cost, and they don't have the time or energy to shop around. In many cases, they're likely to feel dependent on a funeral director to guide them.

What consumers may not realize in their time of need is that just because a funeral home representative is helpful and supportive doesn't mean they need everything he's selling. The funeral business is a $15-billion-a-year industry. Like any business, funeral homes need to make profits. Embalming and caskets are important revenue sources for funeral homes, but they're also not necessary, especially now that green burial is available in more states.

One of the best ways to save money on your funeral is to avoid traditional funeral home services that you don't need. Embalming and "restorative arts" can cost between $700 and $1,000. If you want to have a viewing, use dry ice instead and you'll save enough money for eco-friendly death announcement postcards (500 printed and mailed for you for around $300) and an accordion player to perform the entrance music at your service ($500).

The average casket sale is $2,000 (plus an additional $1,000 to $1,200 for a grave liner, if you're buried at a traditional cemetery). Skip both by choosing green burial, where you can be interred just as you are or in a simple linen, cotton, or silk shroud (you can order a basic burial gown on Amazon for as little as $39, plus shipping), or a biodegradable cardboard casket ($50 to $150) that your friends can decorate at a pre-funeral work party. (Note: green burial grounds do not accept embalmed bodies because the toxic chemicals used pollute the earth. They also only accept biodegradable burial vessels.)

Of course, your survivors won't know they can pick and choose which services and products you want, or that funeral homes aren't the only places to purchase your death merch (there are many online retailers selling caskets, urns, and all sorts of low-cost and eco-friendly burial vessels) unless you arm them with the information they need to be smart funeral shoppers.

The Funeral Rule

The Federal Trade Commission regulates the funeral industry and created the Funeral Rule to protect consumers shopping for death care products and services. Basically, the Rule requires funeral directors to provide consumers with specific information about prices, services, and disposal options. Here are a few of the basic tenets of the Rule:

- In most states you (i.e., your survivors) are not required to use a funeral home.
- Embalming is not required by law, except in rare cases.
- Funeral directors cannot embalm you without permission, and if they do, they cannot charge your survivors for it. (For example, if your survivors say they want an open casket viewing, you will most likely be embalmed unless the person with legal authority to make decisions for you explains that you'd prefer a dry ice pack.)
- Funeral directors must inform you (or your survivors, if you don't preplan) in writing that you have the option of direct cremation or burial.
- Caskets are not required by law, although most traditional cemeteries (excluding natural burial grounds) require a casket, as well as a grave liner or vault to surround the casket. This extra enclosure doesn't preserve the body or the casket. Cemeteries claim they are required in order to prevent the ground from sinking over time. (Whatever!) You are allowed to purchase a vault or liner from an outside source.
- You are not required to purchase a casket from a funeral home. Also, funeral homes are not allowed to charge your survivors a service fee for a casket purchased somewhere else and delivered to the funeral home.
- Caskets, no matter how expensive they are or what they're made out of, do not preserve the deceased. If

a salesperson makes these claims, tell your survivors to wave a copy of the Rule in her face and call foul!

• State laws do not require a casket for cremation, al-

THE PARTY *of* TED KINNAMAN'S LIFE

TED KINNAMAN
1963–
Virginia, USA

EVENT: I haven't really thought about my funeral. I suppose there will be some type of gathering and some words said, but it must be entirely religion-free.

DISPOSAL: I want to be cremated and have my ashes scattered in Lake Mendota at the University of Wisconsin's Memorial Union Terrace. The lake is beautiful, and there's a beer garden, oak trees, ducks, and sailboats. It's my favorite place in the world, and I associate it with being happy and at home. I like to think of my sisters and nieces sitting down for a few beers, then throwing my ashes into the lake.

LEGAL: I already have a medical directive in place, as well as a will.

VIEWS: Burial is such a waste of space. I like the idea of ending up in water; it's symbolic of reunification. It's also the Klingon way, throwing away the body.

though most funeral homes and crematoriums will require one. Providers are required to inform you in writing that you can buy an alternate container (such as a cardboard casket or unfinished pine box) from an outside source and to provide you with containers for purchase.

&. Funeral directors are required to give you an itemized price list in person—or read it to you over the phone, if you request it.

Visit the FTC website (www.ftc.gov/bcp/edu/microsites/funerals) to find out more about the Rule. On the site, you can read (or download) two useful facts sheets, "Funerals: A Consumer Guide" and "Paying Final Respects: Your Rights When Buying Funeral Goods & Services."

You Better Shop Around

The problem with shopping for death merch is that, despite state laws, funeral homes and cemeteries are allowed to make their own rules about how they run their businesses. For example, embalming is not required by law for a viewing, but some funeral directors may balk at arranging a viewing without it. If a funeral director won't arrange your au naturel viewing, take your business elsewhere. Same goes for caskets and cemeteries. If you don't want to pay for a grave liner or casket, choose green burial. With more people interested in personalized memorials and greener exits, many traditional death care providers are adapting to meet demand.

Finally, if you have your heart set an a particular urn, shroud, biodegradable casket, or green burial plot, or want a specific end-of-life provider to handle your exit, make it easy for your team to fulfill your last wishes by leaving instructions, order forms, and a list of your preferred providers and death merch retailers in your funeral box.

Remember, you're in a much better place now than your

survivors will be to identify who can assist your family with your personalized farewell and to research your disposal options. Stressed out shoppers aren't likely to get good deals.

Budgeting Your Last Bash

As you get more involved in your planning, you'll quickly see how expensive it can be to die. That's why you need to set aside a budget for the party of your life, then create a separate body fund to cover the cost of your disposal.

Preplanning is good; prepaying might not be. Visit the Funeral Consumers Alliance website (www.funerals.org) for information on pre-need funeral contracts and funeral insurance. Naturally, you'll want to seek professional financial and legal advice to identify the best end-of-life financial products for your situation.

Here are a few ideas to help you start preparing now for your special send-off:

- Learn about Totten trusts, "pay upon death" bank accounts that provide beneficiaries with fast access to funeral party funds.
- Join a local memorial society that provides members with low-cost cremations and burials. (Google "memorial society + [the name of your state].")
- Make a list of any life insurance policies you hold, or other cash stashes, such as mutual funds or annuities, that may provide death benefits for your family when you perish.
- Check your employee benefits. In 2010, some of the biggest life insurance companies, including MetLife, Prudential, and the Hartford, began offering funeral-planning services as part of employee benefits packages.
- Stop buying expensive coffee drinks. Carry a thermos of homemade coffee and put $3 to $5 in your

funeral savings jar every day. In five years, if you die in a freak accident, you'll have about $3,500 in your jar. That will cover cremation and a fabulous catered funeral dinner for 20 to 40 of your closest friends.

- Send your kids to public school, and instead send that big check to your funeral mutual fund every month.
- Barter. You must have a skill that someone would find useful. Trade it for a sound system, a hand-made pine casket, or a case of gin.

Worst-case scenario: you die suddenly and without funds. Your survivors, because they love you, can hold a fundraiser or two. Enterprising people all over the world have held post-mortem car washes and benefit dinners to pay off their loved ones' funeral debts.

If your team has your plans, knows whom to turn to for guidance and services, and has quick access to your funeral funds, you stand a better chance of getting the funeral you want and deserve.

Start Planning Now

Learn how the system works. Then let your team know, too.

- Download the FTC's fact sheet about the Funeral Rule.
- Visit www.thepartyofyourlife.com for a directory of death merch retailers.
- Store information in your funeral box.

CHAPTER 24

Why Wait?

The Dry Run Funeral

*Y*our guest list is complete, your team members have committed, and you've mapped out your merry memorial down to minute detail. Why stop there? More to the point, why miss the party of your life? Having a dry run funeral is the best way to test your funeral team in action, find out how much your friends and family members really love you, and get the funeral you want and deserve right now.

Your Post-Life Prequel

You've worked hard to plan your exit; aren't you dying for a dress rehearsal? If you're like me and plan on living to 100, that's an awfully long time to wait to be fêted. Plus, if I wait until my "final" funeral, when I'm 100, most of my friends and my original funeral team members will be dead. Then we all miss out.

I want to see what people will wear. I want to hear what

they have to say about me. I want to pile my plate high with edamame snacks and veggie Thai spring rolls, drink plenty of gin, and, most of all, I want to have my vegan funeral carrot cake and eat it, too.

Since you've read this book up to this point, you've had plenty of time to compose a guest list, consider party concepts, craft a preliminary celebration playlist, compile a list of riveting readings and rituals, and create your funeral logo. So, what's the hold-up? You already have the plans. Set a date. Your friends and loved ones are dying to attend.

THE PARTY *of* TRAVIS OLSON'S LIFE

TRAVIS OLSON
1984–
Paris, France

VIEWS:	I want to be the only stiff there; I want this to be a fun thing. If people want to get up and make statements, that's fine, but only if they're not sappy. I don't want a cryfest, although I would like people to feel sad for a while. I want to keep people busy because, if there's just a funeral, once it's over they might feel like they haven't done enough or had enough time to say goodbye.
EVENTS:	I'd like the afternoon to start off with a happy hour where people can mingle and drink enough to get socially lubricated. Next will

Pure and Easy

How much of a dry run funeral you want will depend on a few factors: how much of a party you can afford, how much of a party you think your team can deliver, and how much of your funeral you're comfortable revealing before you die. (Don't think your friends and relatives are above stealing your celebration ideas and dying first.)

You may want or need to downsize or alter your plans to fit into a smaller time frame (and budget). It's probably best to save the weekend funeralpalooza for the real deal and instead,

---

be the Airing of Grievances, where guests can talk about all the things about me that bugged them (and in doing so they'll realize that my idiosyncrasies were actually sort of cute).

THEME:	*Gone with the Wind.*
ATTIRE:	Women in hoop skirts, men in tails (top hats optional).
MAIN EVENT:	Funeral pyre. Once they light the pyre, I want five or six of my women friends, in their hoop skirts, to dance and twirl around the pyre to the Abba song, "Waterloo." I want my ashes to just blow off the pyre into nature. After this, I want there to be a big dance. People will need to block off an entire afternoon and evening for this.
DRINK:	Mint juleps.

condense the party into a single afternoon or evening function. After all, your dry run funeral is a preview of the coming attraction, not the main event.

Also, you might only get your team members and guests to follow your most fanciful plans once, so don't overdo it on your sample send-off. Save the funeral fire-walk for your final farewell. You can still have interactive observances; just keep them simple and lighthearted.

Shine On

Whatever theme you've chosen for the party of your life can work for your dry run celebration, too. However, you might want to replace some of your original readings and rituals with observances that have more relevance to your current state of being.

You're alive! And so are your guests. So, keep your rites focused on making everyone feel good about your life, their lives, and living in general.

Select readings that will inspire your guests to live more simply and more mindfully, or to get over their fear already and take more risks. You can still have a ceremony if you want to. You can still choreograph a special funeral dance and write a catchy funeral tagline. (Note: don't forget to make your life status clear on your party invitation—it's not worth upsetting loved ones with a cryptic missive that could be mistaken for the real thing.)

One of the bonuses of road testing your farewell fiesta: once it's over, you can let go of certain elements of your program. You could still have years or, like me, decades, to refashion your final fandango. You might want to start over with an entirely new concept, menu, decorations, and playlists. You only die once, but who says you can't have a few fantastic funerals before the end? Sometimes it takes a few dry run funerals to get the one you want and deserve.

I advise against combining your dry run funeral with a

milestone birthday. Why dilute either event? You deserve an extravagant birthday bash and a spectacular sample send-off.

Save It for Later

Since you won't be paying for burial or cremation, you can devote all of your pre-funeral budget to the fanfare. Hire a caterer, rent a party room with a view, have a henna tattoo artist on-site to adorn your funeral party (i.e., your funeral team members) so they'll stand out at the festivities. Make place cards for your dry run funeral dinner. Little touches go a long way in making guests feel like they're truly part of the F-U-N.

Don't worry about gift bags for your dry run funeral. You still want your guests to remember you fondly after the party, and they will, but since you'll be alive they don't need mourning gifts. You can celebrate your guests with a single memento, such as a funeral cookie. (In fact, your guest should give *you* presents; you'll need some pampering bath and body products, as well as iPad accessories, for your after-party life.)

If you just can't come up with the funds for a prequel party of your life, get creative. Ask a friend to host a fancy dinner party for you, turn your party into a fundraiser (charge admission and donate the profits to your favorite charity), and research sponsorship opportunities. Your guests might be exactly the demographic a liquor company, organic tortilla chip brand, or local dairy is looking for to promote a new product. (Of course, all of these steps give you the practice you need to hone your budgeting and fundraising skills for your real funeral.)

On the other hand, if money is no object for you or your guests, go ahead and book the weekend "Party of My Life" cruise.

Team-Building Tips

You might be tempted to help your team produce your dry run fun, but don't. Your team needs to make the party of your life happen on their own. You won't be there to hold their hands for the final run, so they need to work out the kinks in the system now while there's still time to learn from their mistakes.

Another reason to hand off the funeral party baton: if, like me, you are likely to live to 100, this might be the only chance some of your team members will get to participate in your funeral. The sad truth is, some of us might die young, and you never know when a loyal and valued team member could fall. So don't rob your posse of this opportunity by interfering or hovering. Trust them to honor you and make you happy.

Hosting a dry run funeral rehearsal dinner is a fun way to build camaraderie among your funeral team members, as well as thank them in advance for their hard work. Why shouldn't your first-tier friends have an exclusive sneak peek at you? A pre-event feast expands the scope of your party without adding much planning and gives you a chance to address last-minute details.

In Case I Die

Finally, you might want to consider what you want your loved ones to do if you should happen to die shortly after your dry run funeral.

Ask yourself:

- Have you been sufficiently honored?
- How much time does your team need to regroup and produce the real deal?
- What if you die just a few days after your dry run funeral?
- Will you mind if people wear the same outfits?
- Would you prefer a different menu this time?
- Do you have a backup playlist?

For me, these are very easy questions to answer: no; three months; so what—I still want my "real" funeral; I won't mind; please add bacon, doughnuts, and Trader Joe's Reduced Fat

Cheese Puffs to the menu; yes, it's in my funeral box, in a folder labeled "backup playlist." The way I see it, your dry run funeral is supposed to be fun, but it's also just a practice farewell. It does *not* count as a real funeral. I still want the full-on program, the weekend of activities. That's why I have a plan B party worksheet in my funeral box.

If you don't plan on living long—or worse, get diagnosed with a terrible disease that will kill you in six months—then the dry run funeral is definitely a spirited and loving way to spend one of your final days. You can still leave plans for your post-death funeral, or leave it up to your loved ones. It's your choice.

(Note: don't dip into the dry run funeral well too many times or you might risk wearing out your funeral goodwill. Wait at least 10 years between dry runs, and it's probably best not to have more than two or three in your lifetime.)

Start Planning Now

There's a lot of down time between major holidays; stir up some fun by announcing your dry run funeral today.

- Consult your funeral team members, and set a date for your practice party.

- Distribute your plans to your team.

- Store information in your funeral box.

Do Before I Die

Your Quickie Party Checklist

Whether you're too close to death to read this book or you just need a little help remembering key planning elements, you can use this checklist to get straight to work on the party of your life. Remember, you don't have to do it all. That's what your funeral team is for!

The Least You Can Do

- ❧ Make a list of everything you do *not* want said or done at your funeral.
- ❧ Assemble a funeral team, or at least recruit a funeral party advocate.
- ❧ Store this information in a findable place, such as your funeral box.
- ❧ Let your loved ones know where your funeral box is.

Here Today, Gone Tomorrow

- Select a disposal method.
- Write down your preferences regarding viewing.
- If you'd like a home-based death vigil and/or funeral, let your loved ones know in advance.

Celebrate Good Times, C'mon

- Describe the type and number of life celebration events you would like.
- Describe your ideal celebration timeline, from death, to disposal, to the party of your life.
- Develop a funeral theme and write your funeral mission statement.
- Make a list of funeral rituals and activities.
- Compile your funeral soundtrack.
- Create a funeral menu, designate a funeral drink, and describe your ideal funeral cookie or cake.
- Create a guest list.
- Store information in your funeral box.

Image Control

- Select the photos you'd like used at your memorial, with your obituary, and for publicity purposes.
- Recruit people to eulogize you, or leave guidelines for your survivors to use in selecting eulogists.
- Prepare information for your obituary (or write your own).
- Design your invitations (or leave instructions with your preferences for paper stock, fonts, etc.) and death notification cards.
- Store information in your funeral box.

A Little Help for Your Friends

- Make a list of professionals (i.e., funeral directors, celebrants, death midwives, etc.) who can help your funeral team with the party of your life and with your body plan.
- Select your officiate, or describe your criteria for an officiate.
- Make a list of preferred burial grounds or ash alternatives.
- Store information in your funeral box.

Budget, Boxes, and Bling

- Research memorial associations and other organizations that offer low-cost burial and cremation options.
- Research funeral merch, such as shrouds, caskets, and urns.
- Make a list of gift bag items.
- Leave a copy of the FTC's Funeral Rule in your funeral box.
- Ask your financial advisor if a Totten trust is right for you.

Start Planning Now!

Acknowledgments

Big thanks to my publisher, Jeffrey Goldman, for his extraordinary patience and for having faith in my crazy sense of humor. Thanks also to Kate Murray at Santa Monica Press for her keen editing skills.

I'd like to thank Kate Rogers, my original agent for this project, for her enthusiasm about my book when I brought it to her many years ago.

I'm grateful to have met during my research many dedicated women and men who are helping usher in a fresh approach to end-of-life matters by educating people about family-directed funerals, green burial, less invasive death care, lower-cost exits, and personalized memorial celebrations. I owe a special thanks to three in particular who generously shared their time and expertise with me throughout this project and provided me with useful feedback on my book: Char Barrett at A Sacred Moment; Nora Cedarwind Young at Thresholds of Life; and Donna Belk of the Crossings Care Circle.

Many others in the biz also kindly took time to answer my questions, explain their work, and direct me to additional resources. I greatly appreciate everyone's input. Thanks to: Cat Saunders at the Heartwings Foundation; John Eric Rolfstaad of the Seattle People's Memorial Association; Jane Hillhouse at Final Footprint; Ruth Faas at Mourning Dove Studios; Joe Sehee of the Green Burial Council; Susanne Wiigh-Mäsak of Promessa Organic AB; Rev. Joellyn St. Pierre; Rene Colson; Jerrigrace Lyons at Final Passages; Elizabeth Knox at Crossings; Cynthia Beal of the Natural Burial Company; and Josh Slocum of the Funeral Consumers Alliance. I enjoyed talking to all of you and always left our conversations feeling inspired and motivated. Change is actually happening in the funeral world, thanks to your hard work.

I wish I'd created the term "end-trepreneurs," which I've used in a few places in the book, but I didn't. Lisa Takeuchi Cullen, author of *Remember Me*, did. Thanks, Lisa.

One of the best parts of researching this book was talking to friends and family members about their final plans. Thank you to the following people for sharing their funeral party ideas with me: Kord Hamilton, Cyrus Farmer, Dana Rourke, Shari Rose, Thom Haslitt, Travis Olson, Ann Woolliams, Chet Haase, Kevin Britten, Ted Kinnaman, Emily Stevens, Bix Skahill, Katie Yates, Gregg TeHennepe, Bill Dewey, Suzan Huney, Amelia Morris Enriquez, Ron Obvious, Nancy Lee, Phil Zrimsek, Becky Loraas Zrimsek, Shirley Whitlock, Steve Clark, Molly White, and my parents, Joanne and Dan Dillman.

Thanks to my friends and family for always supporting my writing and for putting up with my whining when I'm blocked and want to quit. Thanks to my Facebook crew for providing daily, sometimes hourly, crack-the-whip harassment to keep me on track during the final weeks of the project. Your comments really helped. A special thanks to Patricia Welander for her brutally honest commentary and funny anecdotes.

I should thank my funeral team members now, since I won't be around to thank them after they produce the party of my life. THANKS, Emily, Sarah, Brian, Megan, Kamie, Corny, Frank, Kathy, Kate, Shari, Jon, Steph, Marko, Grace, and Katherine. I know you'll do an amazing job!

Finally, thanks to Bruce Michaux, for showing up every day.

♥

Resources

Please visit www.thepartyofyourlife.com for a current, comprehensive list of funeral-related resources, as well as the book's bibliography.

❧ DIY, FAMILY-DIRECTED, *and* HOME FUNERALS

National Home Funeral Alliance
www.homefuneralalliance.org

Home Funeral Information
www.homefuneral.info

Home Funeral Directory
www.homefuneraldirectory.com

Undertaken With Love: A Home Funeral Guide
www.undertakenwithlove.org

❧ HOME FUNERAL GUIDES, DEATH MIDWIVES, *and* RELATED PROVIDERS

A Sacred Moment
Offices in Seattle and Everett, Washington
www.asacredmoment.com

Ceremonies for Life's Thresholds
Port Townsend, Washington
www.thresholdsoflife.org

Crossings.
Takoma Park, Maryland
www.crossings.net

Crossings Care Circle
Austin, Texas
www.crossingscircle.org

Final Passages
Sebastopol, California
www.finalpassages.org

Natural Transitions
Boulder, Colorado
www.naturaltransitions.org

Personal Farewells, LLC
Jefferson, Wisconsin
www.personalfarewells.com

Peaceful Passage at Home
Shirley, Massachusetts
www.peacefulpassageathome.com

Sacred Ceremonies
Webster, Wisconsin
www.sacredceremoniesltd.org

Shiva Sisters
Los Angeles, California
www.shivasisters.com

Thresholds Home and Family-Directed Funerals
San Diego, California
www.thresholds.us

Turning Leaf Home Funerals
Plymouth, New Hampshire
www.turningleafhomefunerals.com

Mourning Dove Studios
Arlington, Massachusetts
www.mourningdovestudios.com

❧ LIFE CELEBRANT TRAINING *and* DIRECTORIES

Celebrant Foundation & Institute
www.celebrantinstitute.org

Insight Books, Inc.
www.insightbooks.com

UK Celebrant Directory
www.funeralcelebrants.co.uk

Funeral Celebrants Association Australia
www.funeralcelebrants.org.au

❧ STATE *and* FEDERAL LAWS

Federal Trade Commission
www.ftc.gov/bcp/menus/consumer/shop/funeral.shtm

National Funeral Consumers Alliance
www.funerals.org

Funeral Ethics Organization
www.funeralethics.org

&. MEMORIAL SOCIETIES

Funeral Consumers Alliance State-by-State Directory
www.funerals.org/affiliates-directory

The Memorial Society of British Columbia
http://www.memorialsocietybc.org

&. FUNERAL CONCIERGE SERVICES

The Funeral Lady
http://thefunerallady.wordpress.com/

Funeral Concierge Services
www.funeralconcierge.com

Everest
www.everestfuneral.com

&. PARTY PLANNING

Lights Out Enterprises
www.lightsoutenterprises.com

Loving Touch Memorial Services
www.lovingtouchesmemorialservices.com

The Celebration Studio (New Zealand)
www.celebrationstudio.co.nz/funerals

❧ ECO-FRIENDLY DEATH MERCH

The Natural Burial Company
www.naturalburialcompany.com

Final Footprint
www.finalfootprint.com

❧ ONLINE FUNERAL PLANNING SERVICES

My Wonderful Life
www.mywonderfullife.com

Funerals To Die For (United Kingdom)
www.funerals-to-die-for.co.uk

❧ ONLINE FUNERAL FUNDRAISING

Give it Forward
www.giveitforward.com

Go Fund Me
www.gofundme.com

❧ PLANNING IDEAS & TIPS

Funeralwise
www.funeralwise.com

The Funeral Site
www.thefuneralsite.com

Funeral Ideas
www.funeralideas.com

❧ FUNERAL-RELATED MEDIA, SITES, BLOGS, *and* PROGRAMS

Obit
www.obit-mag.com

Daily Undertaker
www.dailyundertaker.com

Taphophilia
www.taph.com

POV: A Family Undertaking
www.pbs.org/pov/afamilyundertaking/

Death Reference Desk
www.deathreferencedesk.org

❧ LOGGING OFF *of* YOUR ONLINE LIFE

Deathswitch
www.deathswitch.com

Slightly Morbid
www.slightlymorbid.com

Legacy Locker
www.legacylocker.com

The Bell Tolls
www.thebelltolls.com

AssetLock
www.assetlock.net

❧ GREEN BURIAL *and* NATURAL DEATH: NONPROFIT ORGANIZATIONS

North America

The Green Burial Council
550 D St. Michaels Drive
Santa Fe, NM 87508
Tel: (888) 966-3330
Email: info@greenburialcouncil.org
http://greenburialcouncil.org/

Natural Burial Co-operative, Inc.
14 Division Street
 Guelph, ON N1H 1P9, Canada
http://www.naturalburial.coop/canada/
http://www.forestofmemories.org/eco_burial.htm

Natural Burial Association
70 The Esplanade, Suite 400
Toronto, ON M5E 1R2
Tel: (416) 360-0044
Email: info@naturalburialassoc.ca
http://www.naturalburialassoc.ca/

Great Britain, Australia, New Zealand

The Natural Death Centre
In The Hill House
Watley Lane
Twyford, Winchester, SO21 1QX
Tel: (+44) 01962 712 690
Email: contact@naturaldeath.org.uk
http://www.naturaldeath.org.uk/index.html

Natural Death Care Centre
Byron Shire, Northern NSW, Australia
Email: info@naturaldeathcentre.org.au
http://naturaldeathcentre.org.au/

New Zealand Natural Burials
P.O. Box 41132
Eastbourne, Wellington, New Zealand
Email: mark@naturalburials.co.nz
http://www.naturalburials.co.nz

❧ GREEN BURIAL GROUNDS

USA

Glendale Memorial Nature Preserve
297 Railroad Avenue
DeFuniak Springs, FL 32433
Tel: (850) 859-2141
Email: info@glendalenaturepreserve.org
http://www.glendalenaturepreserve.org/

Ramsey Creek Preserve and
Honey Creek Woodland
Memorial Ecosystems, Inc.
111 West Main St
Westminster, SC 29693
Tel: (864) 647-7798 (office)
Tel: (864) 324-2647 (cell)
Email: kimberley@memorialecosystems.com
http://www.memorialecosystems.com/

Foxfield Preserve
P.O. Box 202
9877 Alabama Ave. SW
Wilmot, OH 44689-0202
Tel: (330) 763-1331
Fax: (330) 359-7898
email: Jennifer@wildernesscenter.org
http://www.foxfieldpreserve.org

Forever Fernwood
301 Tennesse Valley Road
Mill Valley, CA 94941
Tel: (415) 383-7100
Fax: (415) 383-7409
Email: info@foreverfernwood.com
GPS coordinates:
N 37° 52.648'
W 122° 31.409'

Ethician Family Cemetery
1401 19th Street
Huntsville, TX 77340
Tel: (936) 891-5245
Tel: (936) 295-5767
Email: info@ethicianfamilycemetery.org
http://www.ethicianfamilycemetery.org/

Greensprings Natural Cemetery
293 Irish Hill Road, P.O. Box 415
Newfield, NY 14867
Tel: (607) 564-7577
Email: info@naturalburial.org
http://www.naturalburial.org/

Mother Rest Sacred Grove
Gaian Life Church
P.O. Box 3713
Blaine, WA 98231
Email: mrsgrove@premier1.net
http://www.feri.com/frand/Wicca10.html

Honey Creek Woodlands
2625 Highway 212 SW
Conyers, GA 30094
Tel: 770-483-7535
Email: info@honeycreekwoodlands.com
http:www.honeycreekwoodlands.com

White Eagle Memorial Preserve
401 Ekone Rd.
Goldendale, WA 98620
Tel: 206.350.7353
Email: whiteeagle@naturalburialground.com
http://www.naturalburialground.com

Cedar Brook Burial Ground
175 Boothby Rd
Limington, ME 04049-3019
Tel: 207-637-2085
Email: a.green.cemetery@gmail.com
http://greencemetery.blogspot.com/

Steelmantown Cemetery
327 Marshallville Road
Marshallville, NJ 08270
Tel: 609-628-2297
http://www.steelmantowncemetery.com

New Zealand

Wellington Natural Burial Cemetery (Makara)
New Plymouth Natural Burial Cemetery (Awanui)
Tel: 0800 525 500
http://naturalburials.co.nz

Green Burial Lands in Progress

Prairie Wilderness Cemetery
36565 WCR 80
Briggsdale, CO 80611
Tel: 303-832-7074
Email: prairielaina@yahoo.com
http://www.prairiewildernesscemetery.org/

Natural Legacies
Trust for Natural Legacies, Inc.
P.O. Box 490204
Minneapolis, MN 55449
Email: theresa@naturallegacies.org
http://www.naturallegacies.org/

Commonweal Conservancy
117 N. Guadalupe Street, Suite C
Santa Fe, NM 87501
Tel: (505) 982-0071
Fax: (505) 982-0270
Email: ted.harrison@commonwealconservancy.org
http://www.commonwealconservancy.org/